THINK
SPEAK
ACT
STRATEGICALLY TODAY!

A Leadership Story for Human Resources Professionals

NADINE STEAD ONTIVEROS

To my husband, who saw me when I was invisible.

TABLE OF CONTENTS

INTRODUCTION

Today's HR professionals face a pressing challenge: the need to adopt a more strategic approach to their roles. Yet many find themselves at a loss, unsure of what strategic thinking entails and lacking the guidance needed to navigate this transition. HR professionals in small-to-midsize companies, typically strong operational contributors who wear many hats in their role, do not necessarily have access to coaching or mentoring on *how to be strategic.*

In addition, many CEOs and senior professionals struggle to articulate the concept of strategic thinking. I have met with HR professionals who have been at a loss regarding what being strategic means. They do not know how to *become* strategic. The inspiration for this book emerged from these interactions with individuals whose supervisors had instructed them to be strategic without providing any clear explanations or tangible examples of what that should involve.

Of course, conferences may offer high-level frameworks for writing strategic plans. However, these are often too complicated for you to implement by yourself. The challenge remains: How can I embody and practice strategic behaviors?

I believe that being strategic is not as complicated as we think, which is why, in this book, I offer simple, practical tools to help you, as an HR professional, learn to 'become' strategic. This book also conveys the important concept that strategic thinking, speaking, and acting are not either/or propositions: a person does not need to choose between being strategic *or* operational.

Rather, you can be both strategic *and* operational. The best executives of mid- to small-size companies operate effectively in each space and can switch fluidly between the two in their day-to-day work.

Realistically, opportunities for 'strategic-only' roles in small-to-midsize companies are rare. However, an HR leader who can be both strategic and operational is a gift to the organization, and these skills can be extremely rewarding to you as a professional.

In this book, I aim to bridge that gap between the operational and the strategic by providing a comprehensive understanding of what it means to be strategic in three different roles: that of HR professional, HR team leader, and HR organizational leader. Going beyond theoretical concepts, my book will equip you with practical tools to help you evolve into a strategic HR professional.

Throughout the book, you will join three imagined professionals—Louisa, Danielle, and Sam, each on a professional journey in their own fictitious company. We start with how they meet and decide to form a professional support group: their experiences may even inspire you to start your own. You will come to understand their distinct strategic challenges and how they determine their next steps in thinking, speaking, and acting strategically.

As the author, with a background in strategic planning across diverse industries, I bring over 15 years of experience in strategic HR leadership. Having facilitated team and organizational strategic planning, coached individuals, and spoken at conferences, I believe that I'm well-placed to describe the practical application of strategic principles in terms of thinking, speaking, and acting to contribute to and drive organizational success.

The field of HR is continually evolving in response to a changing world. According to the Roman emperor and Stoic philosopher Marcus Aurelius, "The universe is transformation; life is opinion." This neatly encapsulates life's dynamic nature and our response to the flux. Success in HR within this ever-changing landscape hinges on our ability to embrace strategic thinking, acting, and speaking.

If you are an HR professional, now is the time to consider your potential evolution as a strategic leader in your business. This book can be your guide to becoming a strategic force in HR, offering insights on how to confidently show up strategically in your daily and long-term work. I urge you to embrace the transformation—and let strategic thinking propel your success in the dynamic field of human resources.

CHAPTER

1

UNEXPECTED ENCOUNTERS

Meet Luisa

So here I am, looking around nervously, hoping that we'll all be called in to take our seats soon and that I can stop feeling so out of place. Everyone around me looks comfortable in their suits and sharp, professional outfits. They all seem to know each other and huddle in small groups, catching up on the news and most likely discussing their latest strategic successes. They look so "credible."

And me? I'm not aiming for "credibility"; I'm just trying to look relaxed and approachable. But it's clearly not working, because no one has approached me. *This is a mistake,* I tell myself. *What am I doing here? Why am I trying to network with these smart people from successful companies? Do I really belong here?*

Then I remember.

A few weeks back, my CEO had called me to discuss the upcoming expansion of the business. He said my department, HR, would have an important role to play. Our company, We Fix Things, is about to move from our familiar territory of household equipment repairs into a totally new arena—retailing and installation. It's going to require a fast learning curve, and we're all going to have to step up.

I'm excited about this new direction. I love the company. I've grown with it over the years, starting as an admin assistant twenty years ago when it was just a local handyman firm. I completed my business degree while working and raising my family, and I built the HR department from scratch. Eventually, in recognition of my loyalty, the CEO named me Director of Human Resources.

Although I'm proud of my professional growth, I can't help thinking that my boss and other directors think of HR as less important than other areas of the business. Yeah, it's an outdated view. But in reality, getting the new recruits onboarded, handling employee issues for the managers, and organizing regular company celebrations—which everyone loves, by the way—has become my role over the years. I've been coasting, safe in my comfort zone, and I'm yearning for something new.

Now that the business is evolving, there should be much more for HR to do, and many of the ways we work will need to change. Although my team—an HR specialist and my executive assistant, who also serves as general admin for the company—is hard-working, we're already stretched thin dealing with our current workforce of more than 100 employees.

Anyway, when I headed to my boss's office, he got straight to the point. We've known each other for decades, so there was no need for small talk.

"Luisa," he said, "as you know, we're about to grow the company and branch out. It could be the best thing we've ever done, but we're taking a significant risk. The competition will squash us if we're not careful. Customers these days are cynical. People trust us to fix their things—but will they trust us to sell them products that last, or will they soon be paying us to repair them?"

I listened with interest, waiting to see how he wanted HR to contribute to this new direction.

"Procurement and logistics are going to become massively important. I'm going to need the whole team to be more strategic going forward so that we'll all know where we're going and how to get there. I know I can rely on your help."

It may sound cheesy, but my heart leapt in excitement. Finally, here was my chance to step up and be part of this incredible business transformation—even though I needed to know what he envisioned my strategic role to be.

He continued. "So, can you go ahead and book somewhere off-site for an executive retreat in four weeks? I've found a strategic planning consultant to lead the meeting. Let the exec team know where and when. Just make sure everything runs smoothly. And let's make sure the food's good—better than last time, since I don't want the team complaining."

With that, he turned to me in a dismissive way, picking up some papers on his desk as if he was getting back to work. "Thanks, Luisa. I know I can rely on you."

In a nano-second, my heart stopped leaping and just slumped. *Was that really how he saw my contribution to this huge transition?* Is HR merely an efficient department, always ready to help and always prepared to respond to any request—anything *but* a strategic player in the business?

He saw me as "good old Luisa"—capable, supportive, and trustworthy. Even though I'm all those things, on *that* day, I knew I wanted to be something more.

The mention of a "strategic planning consultant" also seemed ominous. If he only saw me playing a support role, would the consultant recommend bringing in someone above me? That's what happened to my colleague Susanna at the Stoneworks Company next door.

Yet, this business transition needed to succeed. I knew the company inside out, and it was time to step up and do—what?

"Sure," I replied calmly, readying myself to step up to the plate. "I'll get my team to organize the retreat details since I'll be preparing the HR contribution to the strategic planning. If we need someone to take notes, perhaps your assistant can do that—because I'll be involved with the team working on the new business plan."

My boss glanced up from his papers and gave me a surprised look but said nothing. I smiled and walked out.

Outside the door, I took a moment to reflect on what I'd just said and done. It felt good. Then I realized what I'd committed to. Transitioning from "cozy and reliable" to "executive team member" in the eyes of my peers was going to take a lot of work. I needed to find some guidance and inspiration, and there was no time to lose.

So, that's what I'm doing here at my first-ever Human Resources Networking event. I'm taking the first step towards reinventing myself as a leader—not just a leader of my small HR team but also a "strategic business partner" for my colleagues and a respected counsel for my boss. I'm impatient to get started.

After what seems like an age, the doors to the conference room begin to open. People drift in and take their seats.

My first instinct is to sit near the back, invisible, so the more worthy ones can take their places in the first few rows. Instead, I think again. *Am I not worthy?* I move to the front and choose an empty seat just off-center.

To my right is a young woman, about thirty. She looks professional and self-assured. After the briefest smile and nod of hello to me, she returns to being immersed in her thoughts. I wonder what brought her here.

Meet Danielle

I hate waiting for conferences to start. The COO's words are still playing in my mind. I know I need to do something, but I don't know what.

My company, We Make Things, is expanding, and we now have several manufacturing sites. More are planned. Since I joined two years ago, my team and I have worked hard to streamline the company's HR processes. Each team member contributed the ideas and suggestions that helped us achieve a transformation, and I'm proud to say that our department is now considered to be user-friendly and efficient.

So, you can imagine my dismay when the COO instructed me to cut one of my team members to save on costs. Which of my four direct reports could I do without? We are such a tight, supportive team. What effect would removing a position have on the morale of the others? What would it say about me as their team leader?

What's worse is that I'd been planning to request an *additional* position to cope with the increasing demands on HR as the company expands. When I explained this to the COO, she responded that she *might* consider revisiting the situation if I could justify the team's roles within a strategic HR plan.

The problem? I have never created a strategic plan before and don't know where to start. As this will "make or break" my team and my reputation as their leader, I have to get it right the first time.

I've only recently been promoted to VP of HR. The title is impressive, but the position only became available because my predecessor left abruptly due to health issues. I was likely just the easy choice. And— let's face facts—it was less expensive to promote me than to recruit from outside.

I guess I still have a bit of "impostor syndrome." They still need to fill my Director of HR position, so I'm still doing the same job as before, only with a slight pay raise and extra responsibilities.

None of this is making my life outside work any easier. I've been staying late at the office and bringing work home, and my partner is not impressed. Any talk of making things permanent between us has faded away. Even my parents, who love boasting about their clever daughter with her MBA and fancy job title, are constantly asking when I'll settle down and start a family.

So, please, let this day's networking with other HR professionals inspire me and give me some fresh ideas. I need to understand how I can *own* my VP of HR title and lead my team successfully to add real value to the company.

I take a seat in the front row between the friendly-looking woman on my left and the sharp-suited man on my right. Now, *he* looks like a real CHRO—confident in his skin, like he's earned the right to be here.

I hope we'll get started soon.

Meet Sam

It's a relief to get away from the chaos at the office and from the never-ending demands of our newborn daughter who always needs to be fed, held, or changed. I adore her, but she's been keeping me awake all night for weeks, making it hard for me to think clearly.

I need to take a few moments to clear the brain fog and think about what I really want to achieve today.

As a military man, I've been on the battlefield and earned respect for my strengths. I understand the benefits of a transparent chain of command. When a superior tells me my objectives and I know the strategy, I've always executed my missions flawlessly, always protecting my men and achieving our aims with minimal losses.

And when I joined civilian life, this disciplined approach served me well. I had no difficulty getting recruited by some big-name companies. Once I specialized in HR and understood the company's expectations,

10

I always succeeded in achieving my goals. That's why I got promoted so quickly through the ranks.

Each time, I'd start with the company's business plan and work on my tactics to align the HR department's processes and budget with the company strategy. I'd remove inefficiencies and implement any required changes. I felt trusted to do whatever was needed for the business to transition to a new way of working and succeed.

My peers and teams respected me for my measured, logical approach. I've always been able to reassure them that I knew where we were going, even when significant changes of direction were necessary to achieve the company's goals.

I was on an upward career trajectory, earning rapid promotions, achieving my goals without fail, and outperforming expectations.

So, when I was headhunted and recently offered the newly established position of CHRO at We Automate Things, a rapidly growing SaaS company with a stellar reputation for innovation, I took it for granted that my success would continue.

But it wasn't long before I realized I'd made a critical error—one that would have cost me and my team dearly if we'd been on the battlefield. I'd waded right in without understanding the complete picture.

You see, I sailed through the interview process smoothly, describing in detail how, in the past, I'd implemented more streamlined processes to reduce costs and increase efficiency. The search committee had loved the sound of that.

Naturally, I'd asked about their 5-year business plan and was assured that it was in place. However, what I'd missed was that "in place" meant that it had been sitting on a shelf, gathering dust, for at least a couple of years. No one ever looked at it, let alone used it to guide their efforts.

Fast forward a handful of weeks, and here I am, at this HR networking conference, looking for a way to climb out of this mess. I've been in the post for thirty days now, and last week, I got the request to propose the departmental budget for next year.

Without a strategic plan, how am I supposed to decide on my priorities? I've reached out to my fellow VPs, but they all have different opinions about what they need from HR. The only thing they have in common is that they see the department as transactional and of marginal benefit to the business. The VP of Ops is even suggesting that the department be dissolved!

I'm feeling my lack of a real foundational education in HR. How can I admit I don't know where to start? If I don't deliver, my credibility with my boss and peers will be destroyed before I've had a chance to show them what I can do.

I need to work on this issue and follow a system to get a budget aligned with the business's needs. I'm hoping that when this conference starts, at least one of the speakers will describe a solution that can help me deliver what's needed.

The lights in the auditorium are dimming, and we're about to get down to business. I need to forget how tired I am and try to focus.

CHAPTER

2

THE PACT

*Friendship is born at that moment when
one person says to another, 'What! You
too? I thought I was the only one.'*

— *C.S. Lewis*

One after the other, each presenter at the conference gives fascinating perspectives on how they have addressed their company's HR people-related challenges and achieved impressive results. Inspiring? Yes—but somehow abstract.

Most members of the audience are busily taking notes or making recordings (believing they will find time to review the information later). However, for our three heroes, the answers they have been hoping to find remain elusive.

Luisa is still waiting for her practical questions to be addressed. She wonders: How can I *"be strategic" to help drive We Fix Things as the company branches out into a new business area? What exactly is strategic thinking? What does my boss mean when he says I need to be more strategic?*

Danielle continues to search for answers about how to lead her HR team to success and achieve her ambition of becoming a CHRO: *How do I align my HR team to the strategic plan? What does a strategic HR team even look like?*

And Sam, who is struggling to find his authentic voice and use his strengths to propel his enterprise forward as it grows, awaits the answers to two burning questions: *How do I lead without having a strategic plan as my guiding light? How can I effectively guide the CEO and executive team to recognize the necessity and benefits of implementing a new strategic plan?*

The lunch break is short—just time to grab a juice and a couple of sandwiches. While some of the more seasoned participants enjoy reconnecting with previous contacts, the newbies are more reticent and eager to return to the business at hand. While they wait, they either hone in on someone who seems alone and make awkward small talk or they head outside for some fresh air and daylight, avoiding the embarrassment of standing alone.

Everyone who's ever been to one of these events knows about the dreaded "after-lunch" presentation slot. No matter how electrifying the presenter or how riveting the subject matter is, the post-prandial lull lowers the energy in the room to close to zero. Rather than adding a sense of drama, the darkened auditorium invites the audience to drift off into a peaceful doze.

Thankfully, the organizers have anticipated this perennial issue and devised a solution—something a little different to wake up the room and to shift the mood from passive to active.

A new speaker, consultant Simone Grant, takes the stage. The first surprise is that she doesn't start by talking about strategy. Instead, her first slide is entitled 'Think, Speak, Act Strategically—Today!'

Well, at least she's grabbed our interest by promising something we can do immediately, Sam thinks.

Grant, who cuts a striking figure in her well-tailored suit and who carries herself with the confidence of someone who has spoken to many large crowds like this, introduces herself—"Call me Simone!"—and explains how she developed the model she's about to present.

"I've been in HR for most of my career, and I truly believe that HR professionals are among the most dedicated in any organization. However, thinking about it, the majority of American companies are small to midsize.

"And let's face it, HR is often the most understaffed department, and it tends to be regarded as a 'cost' rather than a 'benefit.' Even those of us in VP, Director, and Manager roles (our titles are often ambiguous) get stuck in the daily weeds.

"But for us to be truly the most effective," she continues, "we need the mindset of zooming in and out—like a hawk, flying high for the long view and big picture, then landing to advise or implement the close-up, tactical operations."

She pauses and surveys the room, smiling and nodding as she gauges the facial expressions and body language of her audience. Making eye contact with selected individuals, she continues.

"Over the years, I've worked with HR professionals at all levels and in every kind of organization. And recently, they're talking to me more and more about how the role of HR has evolved and is continuing to evolve.

"These HR leaders are now expected to make a strategic contribution to the success of their company—and they're all fired up and ready to get started. They've read the books, and they've watched the videos, but for the most part they haven't found the practical answers they're looking for.

"The number one question I hear is: 'How can I *be* strategic in my current role?'"

She notices the listeners sitting more forward in their chairs, their interest piqued by her question as they hope to hear her response. Her enthusiasm continues.

"That's a big question I used to struggle to answer. I used to believe that the answer was different in every case. Organizational priorities vary, and people are at different stages in their career journeys.

"So, I needed a way to help individuals, regardless of their starting point, find that elusive road map that could answer their questions. That road map would take them from *operating reactively to leading strategically*, making them key players in driving their organization's success."

Simone smiles at the audience, acknowledging their increased attention.

"My first step was to start challenging assumptions about strategic thinking in an HR context. I wanted to dispel the notion that 'I don't need strategy in my role today. First, let me deal with everything piled up on my desk.' Because, for many of us, it's always 'today'—and a 'strategic tomorrow' never comes.

"I also wanted to take a big-picture look at how HR is rebranding itself and how the paradigm is shifting from transactional to transformational. This is backed up by research from leaders in the field—consultants and academics from SHRM, Gartner, and Korn Ferry 3. These are names we've all heard of, even though we don't necessarily imagine their impact on our daily working lives."

She feels the palpable shift in the room's energy as people shake off their post-lunch stupor and start becoming engaged.

Her first slide is a diagram that depicts a cycle: **Think-Speak-Act**.

Simone starts by explaining how these three connected verbs relate to being strategic.

"You may be wondering why I based this model on such simple ideas. But we all know that our thoughts, our words, and our acts are all interconnected, so they make a great starting point.

"How we *think* influences how we speak. How we speak influences how we act. How we *speak and act* is what creates our professional brand.

"Our aim," she continues, "is to align our thinking, speaking, and acting. That way, there will be a connection, a wholeness, in our thoughts, words, and actions. This *integrity of thought, speech, and action* is what will create our personal brand and build trust with those around us. A brand based on authenticity shows others who we are. It's a way of being."

She surveys the crowd. "Okay, I hear you saying, 'That's all good, Simone—but how does all this help me to *be* strategic?'

"Well, *being* strategic is one way of being. It means addressing the challenges and opportunities of the future. When you think, speak, and act strategically—when those things are integrated—they become who you are. Not a mask, a band-aid, or an add-on skill that you learn in a classroom."

She feels the anticipatory energy and senses that the room is still with her, waiting for her to continue.

"Once we decide to align our thoughts, words, and actions, we can ask some compelling questions.

"Let's take the example of an experienced HR professional working in a small company about to embark on a significant change project. However, continuing to work in the same old way—no matter how well it's been working until now—isn't going to cut it anymore. That person is going to need to **be** *strategic*—which, in essence, means answering three fundamental questions."

Her slide presents these questions in a large, bold font:

- ✓ **Where are we today?**
- ✓ **Where do we want to go?**
- ✓ **How will we get there?**

She reads them aloud and continues, "So, for an individual to start this future-facing way of thinking, the three questions will become—" as she points to the next slide and speaks the words:

- ✓ **Who am I today?**
- ✓ **Who do I want to be?**
- ✓ **How do I get there?**

"From there," she explains, "the thinking naturally feeds into speaking: **Am I speaking in a way that reflects how I want to be perceived?**

"To be strategic, I need to show up as an active, not passive, participant in the business. I need to help define where we are today, where we are going tomorrow, and how we will get there.

"So, when we approach 'acting strategically,' the questions become: **Are my actions the outcome of my strategic thinking and speaking? Do I continually learn so I can think, speak, and act (contribute) strategically?**"

Many heads in the audience are nodding in recognition and agreement. Simone feels that they are with her now.

"The kind of future-facing questions someone in this situation could ask themselves might include—," She pauses a moment before talking them through the slide's key points.

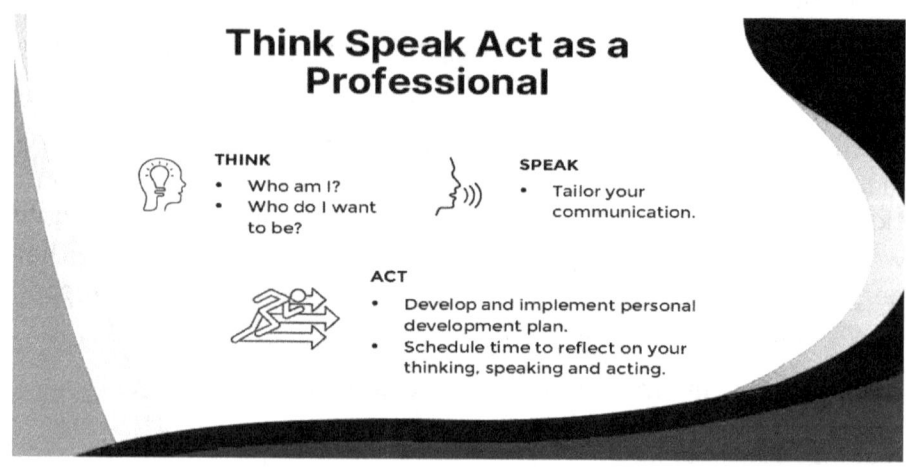

✓ *Think: Who am I? What are my strengths? Who do I want to be?*

✓ *Speak: Ask future-facing business questions. Who do we want to be?*

> *Speak specifically about how you will contribute to the organization's future.*

> When ideas are presented, do you identify risks and opportunities through the lens of business objectives?
>
> *Do you support your speaking with data?*
>
> ✓ *Act: Do you set times on your calendar to reflect on your thinking, speaking, and acting?*
>
> *Do you invest in continually learning your business and the broader trends that may influence its success?*

A murmur of recognition ripples through the room, then the conference attendees turn to their notepads and keyboards to jot down their notes. The speaker continues when heads come back up and turn toward her, expectantly.

"Let's take another example. This is a pivotal moment in many HR careers: the transition from individual contributor to team leader. Can you identify?"

Many heads nod in assent.

"That transition is far more challenging than we often realize. How could the Think-Speak-Act Model help define the questions and actions that could shift the mindset from operational and efficient to strategic and motivational?"

She surveys the room as she allows a few moments for her audience to silently consider answers to her question displayed on the screen.

"Well, first, we need to start by **considering how much we know about the business and its future direction**. If we're not clear, we need to establish that before we go any further.

"From there, we move to **speaking strategically**. The question that follows could be about how well we are communicating the role of the HR team to the team members themselves as well as to the broader business. Are we taking time to step back and ask the right questions that will keep us aligned with the business strategy, or are we stuck in the mode of 'problem solver'—that is, saying 'Tell us what you need, and we'll get it done for you.'

Simone hears murmurs from across the large room and sees participants nodding in recognition.

"Finally, *how are we going to act strategically?* Perhaps the aspect that most new team leaders struggle with is coaching the HR team in its role of helping to meet the company's strategic objectives. How do we help the team refocus its efforts while still ensuring that the routine stuff gets done?

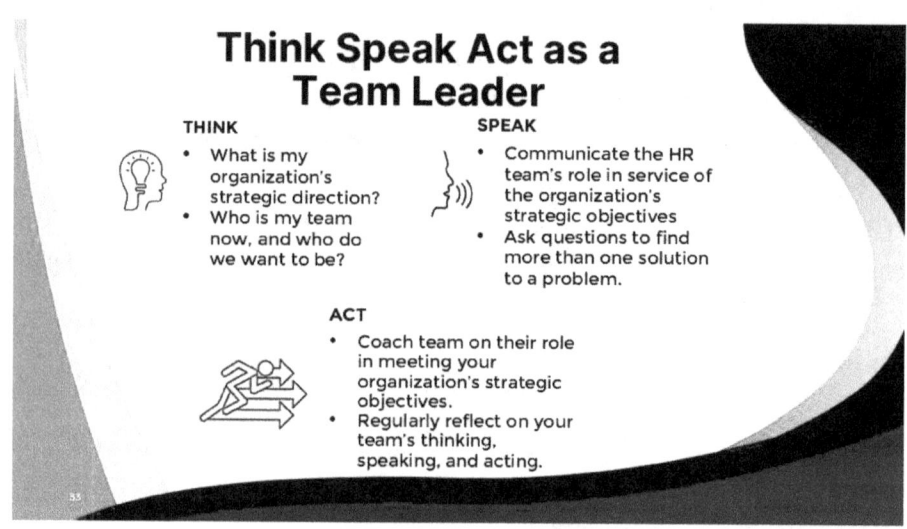

Think Speak Act as a Team Leader

THINK
- What is my organization's strategic direction?
- Who is my team now, and who do we want to be?

SPEAK
- Communicate the HR team's role in service of the organization's strategic objectives
- Ask questions to find more than one solution to a problem.

ACT
- Coach team on their role in meeting your organization's strategic objectives.
- Regularly reflect on your team's thinking, speaking, and acting.

✓ THINK

  How clear am I about my company's strategic direction?

  Who is my team now, and who do we want to be?

✓ SPEAK

  Communicate the HR team's role in service of the organization's strategic objectives

> *Ask questions to find more than one solution to a problem*

✓ *ACT*

> *Coach the team on their role in meeting the organization's strategic objectives*

Most people are taking notes, so she pauses. The only sound is of pens on paper and keyboards tapping as the participants record the ideas on the screen and possibly those inside their minds as they process her advice and think about these significant steps they could take in their own workplaces.

As their heads turn towards her again, Simone resumes. "Is it starting to become clearer now how applying this simple model of Think, Speak, and Act might be all we need to reshape our personal brand and be strategic?"

A sea of nodding heads encourages her.

"As you've probably guessed by now, as HR professionals, you can apply this practical model at every career stage and in every type of organization."

"Let's look at one last example." She turns their attention back to the screen. "Let's go to the top of the career ladder. HR is finally making it to the C-suites of large enterprises. Yet still, all too often, we get the feeling that we haven't really earned our place, that HR isn't integral to creating or driving the business forward. Right?"

She observes many nods, vocal responses, and knowing glances.

"So, what could someone in this position do to become strategic? Just as before, it starts with the way we think, the way we communicate, and the way we act."

A new slide flashes onto the screen.

Think Speak Act as an Enterprise Leader

THINK

- What is important to my CEO, Executive Team and Board?
- Who does the organization need to be to make these priorities realities?

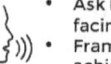

SPEAK

- Ask big picture future facing questions.
- Frame proposals to achieve strategic objectives.

ACT

- Spend time collaborating with key stakeholders
- Regularly reflect on your organization's thinking, speaking, and acting.

✓ *THINK*

> *What is important to my CEO, Executive Team, and Board?*

> *Who does the organization need to be to make these priorities realities?*

✓ *SPEAK*

> *Ask big-picture, future-facing questions*

> *Frame proposals to achieve strategic objectives*

✓ *ACT*

> *Spend time collaborating with key stakeholders*

> *Regularly reflect on your organization's thinking, speaking, and acting*

With all eyes forward toward her, she explains, "As with my other two examples, the first step is to reframe our thinking and reflect on the organization's direction and priorities. **What does the company want, and what will we do to turn that into reality?**

"To start speaking strategically, *go for the big picture*. And don't be afraid to *switch from proposing solutions to working collaboratively* with other key players and asking them the right questions."

In her rhythm, Simone continues. "And to **act** strategically? For me, it often starts with the HR plan. How well does it support the long-term objectives as well as the current priorities? How much input has the rest of the organization had in creating it?

"An enterprise-level HR professional should focus on the overall business thinking, speaking, and acting.

"Is the focus on strategic objectives, firefighting today's issues, or sitting back and enjoying current success? Or are you helping the entire organization stay focused on the challenges and opportunities on the horizon?

"Consider these questions: **How does the organization communicate internally? Is everyone aware of the vision and strategic priorities? Do different areas of the business collaborate well, or do they work in silos, competing with each other rather than supporting and working towards the common goal?**

"At this level, you are taking a 'hawk's view' of the organization's culture, and you need to be ready to lead it in a positive direction so that everyone is united in facing the future."

By now, the room is totally with her.

"The Think-Speak-Act cycle is simple but makes total sense. No complicated theory, no academic background needed. At last, something that can be implemented, starting today. But, to make sure we all know which direction we should be heading when we Think-Speak-Act, here's another slide that makes it clear. As HR professionals, our focus needs to be firmly on the future. Then, we will finally **be *strategic*.**"

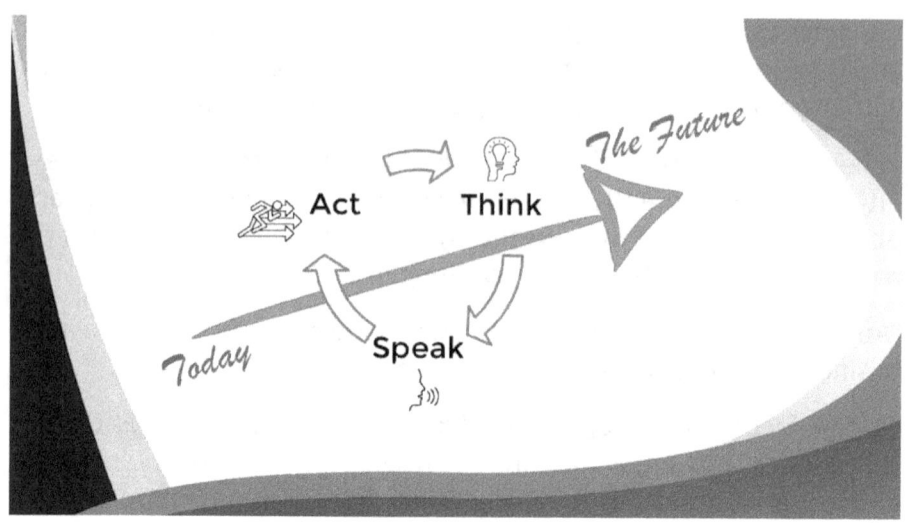

Everyone can feel a palpable eagerness now, as the audience members want to head back to their workplaces and start implementing the model. One closing slide gives suggestions that everyone, regardless of their organization's level, can implement immediately.

The presentation seems to be over, and the enthusiastic applause slowly dies down. But the presenter hasn't finished yet.

"You'll all be returning to work with some fresh ideas from today and ready to try out your new, future-facing way of being. But that doesn't mean that we have to throw away everything we already know.

"So, I'd like to continue this session by introducing you to a simple technique that every one of us can start using today. Before we start, let's take a moment to recognize the value of the collective wisdom and vast experience of hands-on HR in this room. Right now, we're going to harness that body of knowledge to better understand where each one of us is and what we need to do differently to transition to a strategic mindset."

Explaining her use of the Socratic principle of cooperative inquiry—which few of the audience have ever heard of—she describes the structured meeting format she wants us to learn to use. It's an approach to problem-solving that fosters a collaborative atmosphere of thoughtful questioning and exploration.

The first step is for us to cluster into groups of three.

Danielle turns to her left, then right, nodding and smiling at the two colleagues who will now form part of their 'triad.' They smile back in assent.

Next, Simone runs through the rules for the meeting.

"Each group will spend the initial ten minutes sharing brief updates on your respective professional journeys and outlining the specific challenges each of you is currently facing in your companies. This ensures a focused conversation, so you'll understand each other's priority issues."

"Next, we'll shift the spotlight to each individual in turn, granting each of you a focused fifteen-minute slot. What's important to remember here is that *the other two members will refrain from offering direct solutions during this time*—which is not as easy as it sounds! Instead, when you are a listener, you'll embrace the Socratic method and *ask insightful* questions to encourage the presenting partner to explore her or his ideas more deeply."

She clarifies the effect of this approach: "This will create a dynamic of *collaborative inquiry*, allowing each presenter to dig deeper— to unearth, if you will—fresh perspectives and potential solutions from within themselves, guided by the probing questions from their trusted partners."

"This format," Simone promises, "can become a powerful tool for growth and companionship in your careers, a platform where you will find your collective wisdom refined and harnessed to enable you to tackle even your most pressing HR challenges."

Luisa thinks to herself, *Enough theory. It's time to give the Socratic method a try.*

Clustering with Sam and Danielle, Luisa's group agrees to move to the foyer to find more comfortable seating in a corner booth, where they can face each other. As they settle, the three HR professionals introduce themselves. Each one briefly describes the challenges they are facing in their professional and personal lives.

Danielle explains that she's struggling because her COO has instructed her to cut one person from her team. Her company, We Make Things (WMT), is expanding, and the workload is going to increase. She needs to learn how to make a case for expanding rather than reducing her team.

She tells the other two about her career ambitions as well as the pressure from her life partner to spend more time on their relationship. "On top of that, my parents are nagging me to settle down and start a family. How do I juggle it all?" she says with exasperation.

Luisa responds with compassion. "Yeah, I know how your parents might be feeling, as I'm about to meet my first grandchild. I understand where they're coming from. But I can also see your perspective, Danielle. That's a lot of pressure to be under."

Sam steps up to the plate to tell his story. "I'm in a very different situation from you, Danielle, but I'm also frustrated." He explains

26

that he's risen very fast through the HR ranks. "But since being headhunted to join my new employer, We Automate Things (WAT), last month, I've been starting to think I may have made a terrible mistake. Maybe even one that could break my career," he admits. He describes himself as a tactician and an expert at aligning processes to implement and achieve a strategic goal.

"Unfortunately," Sam continues, "WAT doesn't seem to work according to a strategic plan!"

Danielle gasps in surprise. "Really?" she asks. "That must be hard."

"Yeah, and I've never had to create one before," Sam admits sheepishly. "And with a new baby at home and my exhausted wife coping with being a new mom, it's hard to even get enough sleep—much less find the energy to figure out how to work in a space with no plan."

Finally, Luisa introduces herself and explains how her boss at We Fix Things (WFT) sees her role. She describes the upcoming executive retreat and explains how she's hoping to learn how to be strategic rather than just "good ole Luisa in the HR Office."

After ten minutes, the presenter rings a bell and continues moving from group to group, ensuring that each one of the group members gets their chance to speak at length to discuss their situations in more detail.

For almost an hour, the three exchange stories about their adventures in HR: wins and losses, laughter and sighs. As each speaks in turn, the others ask relevant questions and occasionally insert their affirmations in response.

"That felt good," Danielle says after telling Sam and Luisa about her work issues and getting their supportive responses. "By reflecting on your questions, I feel like I'm actually understanding *my* issues better. There is such fun companionship in being understood."

Sam and Luisa smile and reply at the same time. Sam stops to let Luisa continue: "You know, I don't think any of us expected it to be so hard to listen, even for fifteen minutes, without offering advice and solutions to the one speaking!"

"Absolutely!" Sam adds. "It's amazing how much we're learning about each other and ourselves in such a short time."

"Of course, our issues do still remain," Luisa notes wryly. "But I'm starting to feel like a light has been turned on." As they continue to chat, she feels herself starting to understand how much the helpful effect of probing from two peers, even though they are at very different life and career stages, might help her analyze her own situation and work out how to think, speak, and act like a leader.

When Simone announces that time is up, the three group members— previously strangers but now feeling like comrades-in-arms—thank each other, and everyone drifts back into the main auditorium.

Simone turns to the room and invites feedback on the triad experience.

Danielle amazes herself by raising her hand and asking, "The probing questions were so valuable. How can I break the habit of giving advice instead of probing with further questions?"

She hears a ripple of laughter through the room, but she knows people are laughing in sympathy and recognition. *It feels good to be the spokesperson for others.*

Simone smiles and says, "It will be up to each group member to keep the others on track. It gets easier with practice, and once you see that asking the right question is such a powerful tool in strategic thinking, it will eventually become natural for you."

That's why, instead of ending the day exhausted and with a sheaf of notes I'd never have the time to look at again, I'm feeling energized and confident, Sam thinks.

As the three new colleagues say goodbye to each other, they all agree that they've learned something to answer the questions they'd each brought to the conference.

"Now I understand what 'strategic thinking' is in principle—changing my mindset from focusing on the daily tasks to facing the future and supporting the business by ensuring that everything we do is aligned with what the business needs," Luisa exclaims, feeling empowered. "That Think-Speak-Act model has given me lots of ideas about how I can be more strategic by changing how I speak and act. I just need to put it into practice now!"

"Yes, that's so true," Danielle agrees. "As I told you, I've been searching for answers about how to successfully lead my HR team despite needing to cut one of my team members. This model has given me a hint that a road map exists that can enable me to transition from operational to strategic team leadership. It's a guide to stepping up and rebranding oneself."

Sam is standing up straighter and feeling more confident than he had been earlier in the day. "You know, I've really been struggling to find my authentic voice and use my strengths in my new job. I agree that this is a helpful model. I think it can show me how to lead—even without a strategic plan in place in my company."

Luisa speaks up. "Hey, guys. Before we leave today, let's make plans to continue this conversation! Can we find a time next week when we can all get together again?"

Her partners reply with enthusiasm, pulling out their calendars and finding a time and place convenient to all.

"Okay then," Danielle says. "We've made our pact to help each other, and it's up to us to stick to it. Given what we've already shared, none of us had time to lose!"

"Fantastic! See you then! Take care!" Sam and Luisa reply as they each head out in different directions.

CHAPTER

3

BE MORE STRATEGIC!

The only person you are destined to become is the person you decide to be.

— *Ralph Waldo Emerson*

Luisa takes the plunge

I've been excited about our upcoming first get-together. Sam had offered to book us a meeting room at his company's shiny new HQ, but we quickly realized that being in his own workplace could be distracting for him, so we settled on a coffee shop within easy reach for all three of us.

At 9:30, the shop is still quiet, and we settle into a secluded corner with our drinks. Sam even brought a portable whiteboard along.

We'd agreed to stick to the Socratic model of inquiry for our meeting format, and this first week, the spotlight will be on me to start with. This feels a little scary because Danielle and Sam seem so much more self-assured than I do, but I'm prepared to go through a bit of discomfort to get the guidance I need.

We use the first ten minutes to share brief updates on our professional lives and to outline our specific challenges.

Danielle's struggle continues to be about how to be a strategic leader for her team so that it might be seen as an essential contributor to her company's success.

Sam's hope is that our conversation might help him navigate through the unfamiliar territory (for him) of a business without any clear direction or alignment.

And I need some help figuring out what it means to "Be more strategic" so I can prepare effectively for the planning meeting—and leverage my experience to play a valuable role in my company's evolution.

Once we all understand each member's priority issue, we feel ready for a focused conversation around the common theme of strategy.

I take the spotlight first. Inhaling deeply, I launch into my story.

"I'm at a crossroads. WFT is about to branch out and expand beyond our traditional service of fixing household appliances, moving into the sales and installations of new ones. This shift towards a broader market is a huge step for us, which is why our CEO is bringing in a strategic planning expert. He says that successful planning and execution will require a different way of working than how we have worked the past 20 years."

Danielle breaks in with the first Socratic question. "And how did he describe the new way of working?"

"That's just it," I respond. "He didn't explain anything about what he wanted, other than to say we've got to be *'more strategic'*."

Danielle leans forward, her eyes reflecting empathy and curiosity. "Luisa, it sounds like this expansion is going to bring about a huge wave of change. What specific concerns do you have about this transition?"

I sigh heavily. "In three weeks, we'll be having an executive retreat, and the consultant will be leading the meeting. I'm the longest-serving member of the exec team, and I've known the company since Day One. I'm sure I have a valuable contribution to make, if I'm given a chance.

"However, I've known people in similar situations who got passed over for promotion when their boss brought in an external HR professional. It's left me feeling anxious about my future at WFT. I want to prepare myself so that my boss will see me as a business partner and an active contributor to the new plan."

Sam's brows furrow. "I can imagine how that uncertainty could be unsettling, Luisa. But what does 'being strategic' mean to you, and how do you see it aligning with WFT's expansion?"

I hesitate, searching for the right words. "That's part of my struggle, Sam. I don't have a clear grasp of what 'being strategic' means. It feels like an abstract concept, and the future is so uncertain. I need to gain more understanding to contribute effectively to this expansion."

Danielle turns towards me. "Louisa, it's completely normal to feel apprehensive when faced with such a significant shift. You've built the HR function from the ground up and have been an integral part of building the company to where it is today!" she exclaims. "You should be proud of your achievements and shouldn't be worried about your job!"

While I appreciate Danielle's vote of confidence, somehow, I'm not reassured.

"Questions only," smiles Sam as a gentle reminder. "Let's stick to the questioning structure that we saw in the conference. Perhaps the question should be: How and why did you build the HR function from the ground up?"

"To start, there were only ten of us—the CEO, his secretary, me, and the technicians' team. I looked after the administration and bookkeeping and anything else that needed doing. I'm an organized person, and I enjoy taking care of the details so the company can run smoothly.

"As we grew, an accountant took over the finance side. I focused mainly on the 'people' stuff—getting the salaries paid, recruiting new team members when the managers agreed with the CEO that we needed them, dealing with employee grievances, and always organizing an awesome end-of-year party to celebrate a successful year."

While I pause to reflect on what I've just shared, Danielle breaks the silence: "I think that mirrors the career path of lots of people in HR who've found themselves in the profession after starting with a small company that's grown."

Sam interjects calmly, "So, Danielle, can you turn that into a follow-up question for Luisa?"

Danielle, smiling because she's strayed off the path again, pauses. After a brief "Sorry!" she formulates her question. "How are you seen in the company today, Luisa? What is your role right now?"

I take a moment to reflect. Sam and Danielle resist the urge to jump in with another question. I respond carefully.

"I'm seen as good old, capable Luisa, who's been with the company forever. Always ready to help. Just tell me your problem and, no matter what it is, I'll iron it out for you. I'm there to support whatever the exec team or the unit managers tell me they need. I'm there to listen to the most junior employee complaining that their manager doesn't like them. Although I'm on the exec team, they don't treat me as a true business partner. I feel as if they see me as not quite as capable as my peers."

My voice trails away. I frown as I realize, *What I've just described is not what I want my "brand" to be.*

Sam probes further and gently asks, "So, how exactly do your peers treat you, to make you think they don't see you as their business partner?"

I clear my throat and sit up straight. "In meetings, I'm never asked to lead or propose anything new. My role is to listen to what the others are saying and to respond with an offer of help if they need anything from me. They seem to think me capable of carrying out orders given by the key players who are closer to the business and who drive our success. I'm on the sidelines. My role is to react and support."

I'm shocked that I'm saying these uncomfortable truths out loud. I continue, surprised by the pent-up resentment I hear behind my own words:

"And, of course, my boss has relied on me since Day One. Through the years, I've done everything I've been asked, all the while raising my family and even going back to school to get my business degree. I've implemented plenty of new systems and tools in response to real-time situations, so he should know what I'm capable of.

"But when he told me about the strategic planning meeting, he talked to me as if my role was solely to organize the details. No mention of how valuable my contribution will be. To be honest, I've had enough of being seen as his glorified personal assistant."

Danelle asks, "What do you think has contributed to the way you're perceived?"

Now, this is getting a little uncomfortable, but having expressed all these details, I realize that I have to acknowledge some facts. I shift in my seat.

"I guess that, for many years, how I acted worked fine for me and the company. I enjoyed my reputation for being the go-to person for whoever needed help. I enjoyed being busy, and I never said 'no' to any request. Whatever problem you came to me with, I'd fix it for you.

"And I'd even make sacrifices. Last year, the admin assistant I shared with the CEO had to be away from work for a couple of months. So, I asked my HR specialist to take on the CEO's admin tasks. To help her cope with the new workload, I took over some of her routine work. She wasn't impressed with my solution, but still, between us, everything got done. I put in extra hours to keep on top of things. Sadly, my boss didn't seem to notice. My family sure did, though."

Danielle nods and looks at me with consternation. "Yep. The thankless role of the self-sacrificing employee."

Sam asks, "So, since you mentioned that it's your main concern right now, what's your role going to be at the strategic planning meeting?"

"I'm sure everyone will expect me to act the same old way: to listen, to be told how things are and how they're going to be, and to respond by offering to do what's needed.

"In fact, I was pretty proud of myself when I ruled out the idea (that I'm sure my boss had in his head) that I'd be responsible for taking and distributing the meeting notes. He looked shocked when I said someone else should do it as I'd be too busy contributing to the plan."

Even as I'm talking, a new thought is forming, and I continue. "You know, I'm starting to realize that the way I'm seen in the company is actually *a reflection of how I behave*. All these years, I've been setting people's expectations through my words and actions. *And how I behave is a reflection of how I think.*"

Lightbulb moment! That's quite a shift in just over five minutes.

But Sam has a question relating to my previous answer and has patiently waited until I'd followed my train of thought to the end before exploring further.

I turn to Sam, who nods and says, "You mentioned just now that you've implemented programs and tools to solve problems in real time that have helped the company grow. Can you share any previous instances where you successfully applied strategic thinking in your role at WFT? What were the outcomes?"

I struggle to come up with something. "For example, as we began growing, I implemented a CDL compliance program for current employees. As we've taken on more and more people, it became incredibly time-consuming. So, I recently implemented a platform to track all CDL compliance components. It's much more streamlined and efficient now," I say proudly.

Daniele jumps in, "It sounds like you evaluated where the company was and where it was going to determine which initiative to implement. Am I right?"

"Yes, I guess you could say that."

"Do you think that your decision to implement the CDL program leveraged strategic thinking?" smiles Sam.

I've got it! "Right!" *Something just clicked.* "With the CDL, first, I evaluated the situation. We had outgrown the tools we were using. Then, I wanted something that would track compliance efficiently and accurately and that we could scale as the company grows. So, I did my research, identified the best platform for our needs, and implemented it.

"Thinking strategically means evaluating where we are, knowing where we want to go, and determining how to get there," I exclaim with a new sense of understanding.

Sam and Danielle congratulate me. We all smile and take a moment to enjoy this breakthrough.

I'm excited now and ready to continue.

Sam makes a suggestion. "Instead of moving straight on to talk about what your HR strategy is going to look like, why don't we, for the moment, focus on your immediate concern. *How are you going to become a strategic participant at the upcoming planning meeting?* And what will you do to shift the way you're perceived so that you can make and be recognized for your contribution to an effective plan?"

I nod and smile. "Yes, I like that. Let's keep it narrow for now. I know where I want to get to, and I want to leave our session today knowing what actions I can take to get me there."

Danielle gets the ball rolling. "What are the most important steps you can take to 're-brand' yourself as a core member of the strategy team?"

This takes some thought, and I'm hesitant. "I want to start with the exec team. They need to see me as their business partner, as someone who has an important contribution to make."

Sam probes a little. "How can you start changing your peers' perception of you?"

"Hmm. I'm just thinking about what the CEO said. We'll all have to get more strategic—not just me. The first thing I should do is schedule one-on-ones with each exec to explore how they are approaching the expansion, their concerns, and what they currently think they'll need from HR as we go forward."

Danielle asks, "Doesn't that sound as if you're still taking a supportive role?"

Hmm. I take a moment to clarify my thoughts. "I suppose it could be seen that way. But, you see, I never take the initiative like this. My aim now is to arm myself with facts about the business challenges and opportunities that lie ahead for them. I'm typically not part of those discussions. I want the team to expect me to ask business questions and challenge them. I guess that asking questions about the future is part of my learning to '***be*** strategic.'

"It's also clear that we have significant capability gaps, and I'd like to know more about that to get a picture of their expectations of HR's contribution. It doesn't mean my priority will be to meet all those expectations, but I'll be able to consider them before the meeting and propose alternatives if that will help the business more."

Again, Sam urges me to delve a little deeper. "That will get you a mountain of information you can use to prepare for the future, Luisa. And it will start to position you as an active contributor to the expansion. I'm interested that you mention potential 'capability gaps.' What kind of things do you mean?"

I jump in. "Well, for the launch to go well and get the new operations off to a flying start, it's obvious that we're going to bring in some serious marketing and PR. We have a marketing assistant right now, but we'll definitely need someone with the background and skills to plan and execute a successful launch.

"It's the same with Sales—we're going to require a whole new team in place to get the customers to choose us over our competitors and bring in those orders. And in Customer Service, currently, we have a small team taking calls and responding to emails, but will we need to expand the team—or should we outsource? Or use AI? And then, who's going to train and supervise the new installation team? How will we handle logistics?"

I'm breathless. I stop myself and laugh. "A few minutes ago, I thought I'd gotten this all worked out. Now, I see that I don't even know where to start. I'm completely lost again!"

Sam knows the right thing to say. "It's natural to feel overwhelmed, Luisa, but you don't have to solve everything here and now. You've already started to position yourself, even ahead of the meeting, as a business partner with your peers. You've also started to realize what it's going to take to get the company where it wants to be—and the complexity of the transition. Do you think that's plenty for now?"

I laugh. "I guess so. But can I tell you what else I'm definitely going to do?"

They both smile and nod in assent. "Do tell!" Danielle laughs.

"I'm going to request a meeting with my boss—with the time blocked out on his schedule so he won't get called away. Then, I'm going to ask him to brief me on what he sees as the *three most critical business priorities for a successful expansion*. Not HR tasks, but his priorities for the business. With that information and that of the exec team, I'll have an overview and better understanding of how well his and the team's current thinking are aligned."

"Awesome," says Danielle before quickly switching back into Socratic inquiry mode. "Is there anyone else who could help you prepare for the meeting?"

I think for a moment before replying, "Yes, there is! I'm going to contact the strategy consultant to request the agenda and any supporting information. In fact, I could ask them to recommend some additional resources for me to use to prepare for a meeting of this kind because it's new for us."

"That's a bold move, Luisa," says Sam with an admiring smile. "It takes courage to be so open and authentic, especially with someone you don't know. In addition to getting some advance information, are there other benefits in doing this?"

Now, I'm hitting my stride. "Definitely. Before we even meet face to face, I'll have communicated that I won't be sitting on the sidelines as a passive observer ready to be told what to do. I'll be communicating the fact that I'm expecting to be a key contributor, open to change and ready to adapt to new ways of working—and that I'm actively seeking ways to learn, in order to help drive the business forward."

Before I get too carried away, Danielle brings me back to HR reality.

"Everything you've said is valid, Luisa. Grabbing the initiative and reaching out to other stakeholders is a powerful way to start your personal 're-branding'.

"But I do have a practical question for you. You're already busy with your regular work, so how are you going to find the time for all these extra meetings, the external research you want to do, and the prep for this all-important planning session?"

Hmm. She has a good point. How do I resolve this? After some reflection, I speak up. "Let's say I'll need twelve hours for the one-to-ones, four hours to read through the pre-meeting brief in detail, and some additional time to research. So, over the next three weeks, I need to free up my time and stop dealing with everything that comes up and everyone who wants to talk to me.

"First, I'll brief my HR specialist and the admin assistant and ask for their support in handling some tasks I can delegate to them—and I'll share why this is important for all of us.

"Next, *I'll block out my schedule for 90 minutes daily* to ensure that I have time to do what's most important right now and book the one-to-ones in advance. If anyone cancels on the grounds that they're 'too busy,' I'll propose that we have lunch and talk as we grab a bite to eat. These meetings will not be optional.

"Oh, and one last thing. I don't want to pre-empt the planning process, but it would help me if I could gain a greater understanding of the transition journey—from a cultural as well as an HR point of view. So, I'm going to reach out via our local HR networking group and ask if anyone who has already gone through the experience would be willing to meet and share their insights with me."

I was going to leave it there, on a really high note, but Sam has one last question for me.

"I don't want to end on a downer, Luisa, but as we're exploring, I think it's valid to ask: What if you do nothing? What if you go back to the office, get busy with day-to-day issues, and *never find time to be strategic?*"

That question out of left field is certainly thought-provoking. I ponder it for a moment before replying. "What I've realized as I've been answering your questions is just how important *what I think is*. If I believe my role in the upcoming meeting is only to listen, then, of course, I'll turn up unprepared, sit silently, and take notes. I'll be given my instructions and hope that HR can deliver. I'll be called into my boss's office, and he'll tell me that I should prepare for the arrival of the new VP of HR, to whom I'll be reporting in the future, and who will lead the strategic direction of Human Resources at We Fix Things. Of course, he'll reassure me that my contribution is invaluable, and he knows, with my knowledge of the company, how much I'll help her as she takes over the reins."

I stop and take a breath. After a long pause, I raise my eyes and meet their gaze.

"But don't worry. *That's never going to happen*. Because I'm going to do what it takes to **be** strategic and take on the role I need. I owe it to myself, my team, and the company I love. To make the change I want and transform the way I'm perceived, everything starts with *how I think*. With the stories I tell myself about my role. I need to change my story so my mindset shifts toward what I want to achieve in the future. Then, it's natural that how I speak and act will also change.

"That's what the Think-Speak-Act model meant that Simone Grant discussed at the conference. When I start thinking, speaking, and acting strategically—when those three things combine authentically—I will actually **be** strategic.

Danielle and Sam clap their hands, smile, and nod in agreement as my segment of the meeting concludes.

I'm feeling energized, realizing that I'm seeing strategic thinking as a practical tool to navigate the complex landscape of WFT's expansion.

The Socratic inquiry process we've been following has provided me a space to voice my concerns and receive valuable insights from my peers. Together, they've helped me unravel the concept of strategic thinking, demystifying it and empowering me to approach the challenge with newfound confidence.

Little did any of us know that this exchange would mark a pivotal moment in my professional journey, setting me on a path of strategic growth and personal transformation.

Reflections for the Reader

1. THINK

- ✓ How am I perceived in my company? Does my boss see me as an active contributor or a passive supporter? How do I fit into my peer group, and what is my role?
- ✓ What is the most pressing business challenge or opportunity facing my company today?
- ✓ How involved am I in helping to set the direction that will create a successful and sustainable future for my company?
- ✓ How would I like to be seen by my boss and my peer group?

2. SPEAK

- ✓ Does the way I communicate reflect how I want to be perceived in a professional setting?
- ✓ Do I ask future-facing questions of organizational leaders and propose solutions that create the organization's future state?
- ✓ Do I prepare carefully for meetings and clearly understand what I want to achieve by participating?
- ✓ Do I speak with confidence and conviction in meetings, knowing that the situations I describe and the solutions I propose are based on logic and sound data evaluation?
- ✓ Do I actively listen to others and ask probing questions to understand fully?

3. ACT

- ✓ Do I regularly schedule time to reflect on my thinking, speaking, and acting? In a packed calendar, how much time is realistic?
- ✓ What steps do I take to ensure that I'm continuously learning?

✓ What steps do I take to collaborate with other subject-matter experts within the company and learn from them?
✓ How often do I make time to network with my peers in other organizations, share ideas, and learn from them?

CHAPTER

4

TEAM ALIGNMENT?

*A leader is one who knows the way, goes
the way, and shows the way.*

— *John C. Maxwell*

Danielle tells her story

"**N**ow it's your turn, Danielle," Sam smiles, and I'm ready to
begin my story.

*By the end of Luisa's session, we were all pumped by her
breakthrough in strategic thinking and her plan to act strategically to
rebrand herself as a critical contributor to a successful expansion. I'm
hoping they can help me resolve my dilemma.*

Luisa guides the conversation with a gentle question. "You've already
explained that you've been asked to cut one person from your current
team. Maybe you could start by describing your team members'
current roles."

This one is easy. "Sure. I have four people on my team. They're all
competent and committed to HR and the company.

"As you might expect, we have a Talent Acquisition Manager, Laura, whose role is to attract and hire the right people. She manages the end-to-end talent acquisition process, including sourcing, interviewing, and onboarding. I brought her in soon after I joined, and she's been with us for just over eighteen months.

"She works closely with Josh, our Compensation and Benefits Specialist, who designs and manages our compensation structure. He also administers benefits programs and conducts market research to ensure that we remain competitive. Like me, Josh is a business graduate, and although he's only been in the role for a year, it's clear he's very ambitious about climbing the HR ladder.

"Then, there's Mike, our Employee Relations and Compliance Specialist. He's been with the company for over ten years, focusing on maintaining positive employee relations. Mike handles employee concerns and facilitates conflict resolution. He also makes sure we comply with labor laws, regulations, and company policies.

"Last, Anna, our HR Generalist/Coordinator, has been with the company for seven years. She started in general admin but was attracted to HR and joined the department four years ago. In addition to payroll, she handles the day-to-day operations and has recently taken on employee engagement projects.

Luisa and Sam have been jotting down notes. Now Luisa sets down her pen and turns back to me. "Thanks for those details, Danielle. And what about you? What does your role involve?"

That one is more complex. "My title is VP of HR, but I'm only in the role because the previous VP had to leave suddenly for personal reasons. Before that, I was HR Director, and my role was to optimize the company's people processes. I was happy to get promoted; it's great to have the VP title and join the exec team, but nothing much has changed. The HR Director's post has been put on hold, so I'm still doing pretty much the same stuff I did before."

Luisa starts off with the Socratic method. "How is that making you feel? How are you regarded by your new peer group?"

"I'm frustrated, frankly. With my educational background and career progression so far, I've proven I'm capable of growing into the VP role and helping drive the business's success and sustainability. I want to be treated as an invaluable team member by my peers and respected for how I leverage my team's capabilities and encourage them to step up and take accountability. And I'm excited to work out how to make the transition.

"Success in my current role is an important stepping stone to achieving my ultimate career goal, which is to become the CHRO in a major corporation—especially one going through a significant transition. So, I've got a lot to learn and achieve as an HR leader before I settle down and start a family like everyone is urging me to do!"

Now it's Sam's turn.

While we were questioning Luisa, I'd realized that although he gets to the heart of the matter quickly, he also likes as much information as possible to help him direct his questions.

"How are you currently leading your team?" Sam asks.

I pause for a moment to consider an answer. "Well, as each one has plenty of experience in their specific area, I wouldn't say I micromanage them. I make sure they update me on progress and let me know if they encounter roadblocks. If they get stuck for any reason, they come to me, and I try to get them to suggest ways of moving forward. This usually works pretty well. We have a great relationship, and they often suggest ways we can improve our processes. And, since I've arrived, the reputation of the HR department for being responsive and efficient has improved a lot.

Luisa explores a little further. "So, what are the key operational challenges you are facing with your HR team?"

"Oh, everything is working smoothly on a day-to-day basis. But unless I find a way forward, that could all be about to change. As I've mentioned, in our last meeting, my COO told me that he was expecting me to lose one of my team members as part of a wider cost-cutting program.

"Each member of my team has a specific area of expertise, so it wouldn't be just a case of distributing one person's workload to those who remain. The company is still growing, so there will be lots more work for HR, not less, and I'd been planning to request an additional position.

"Right now, the whole team structure is at risk of breaking down. Not only that, but what message will I be sending to the others—about me as their team leader and about the company? I've just got to find a way through this so that the team will become stronger, not weaker, and so that I can really think, speak, and act like a VP, focused on the big picture, and not spend my time getting drawn into routine issues."

Sam gets me back on track. "Are the cuts to the HR team a done deal? Is there anything you can do to reverse the decision?"

"No, not quite a done deal. My COO did tell me that if I can justify my team roles by aligning with company strategy, he *might* consider revisiting his position." I laugh. "That's what led me to be sitting next to you guys at the conference."

Sam and Luisa glance at each other. It's time to delve deeper.

Sam starts. "So now we're moving on to strategy, facing the future. What is your understanding of WMT's strategic objectives?"

"The company has some goals for the next three years. Um, increasing efficiency. Sales targets. And, um, manufacturing." I trail off, embarrassed that I don't know the details, though I've seen them in presentations often enough. "For the most part, they haven't seemed very relevant to the work we do in HR. My focus has been on increasing efficiency."

There's a pause while all three of us consider the implications of my vagueness.

Luisa takes up the thread with a loaded question. "Okay. So, Danielle, how aligned would you say the current HR team activities are with the broader strategic goals of the organization?"

47

I hesitate, then start slowly. "Well, to be honest, *I don't think they are*. We've been doing what every HR department is expected to do: getting people on board, making sure they're paid properly, helping them to have a good experience with our company, and replacing them when they leave. We do all those things well.

"But now you're asking me—and if I can't even tell you the company's strategic goals, how could we be aligned? My honest answer to your question is a confession: I've been focusing on making sure that day-to-day HR operations run smoothly, but I haven't aligned my team's activities to support achieving WMT's business goals. At all."

It had taken almost no time to get to the root of my problem.

"I've been so focused on leading an efficient operation that I've neglected the strategic aspects that are an essential part of my new VP role," I admit, a bit ashamed by this new recognition."

Luisa smiles. "No need for a 'confession,' Danielle, you're doing great."

Leading on from my revelation, she prompts me with a practical question. "What steps will you need to take to transition from this operational focus to becoming a strategic leader? Will the Think-Speak-Act model apply?"

I consider her question for a moment then start formulating an approach.

"The first thing, when I return to the office, is to revisit the company's three-year business plan. I can see it now. The heading is 'Elevate Organizational Excellence and Growth.' It's very vague, and I've never thought much about what that means, like: What actions will we need to take to achieve that? And it's not that I haven't read the contents, because I have. But it was developed between my predecessor's leaving and my promotion, so there's not much related to HR."

Sam raises an eyebrow. "Nothing?"

"Well, as I remember, only when it touches on the department's needing additional manpower. There are no specific HR sections or actions."

Luisa leans forward. "As the plan is already in place now, and HR isn't seen as central to the process, how will that help you become more strategic?"

"I'll go through it in detail and consider the implications of each plan section—not just for HR but for the impact on the business. I *think* there are five goals—I need to re-look at the details. Then, I can consider the role HR will need to play in achieving each one. Some goals will be more 'people-focused' than others, and I'll need more support from my team to achieve them. That will help me define our roles in the future. We may need to change how we work.

"But by understanding the company's aims for the next three years and targeting all our efforts to help achieve them, I can transition the department from purely operational to one that is future-facing and integral to the business's overall success."

Luisa continues her theme. "Okay, you're going to shift your focus to the company's business plan. But I'm guessing that you and your team are already kept busy running an efficient operation. So let me ask a question you asked me earlier, an important one. *What practical steps are you going to take to bring about this change?*"

I pause for a few moments to reflect. "The first step will be to shift my mindset and let go of the day-to-day details. I'm going to have to think differently about what a good use of my time is. I'm going to have to let the team know that they'll have to take accountability for their section and only update or consult me about things that affect our progress toward departmental objectives."

That all feels good.

Sam wants me to add more detail. "Luisa made a lot of great points about how she is perceived by her peers. Do you have any work to do in that area?"

I nod. "I guess so. I need to arrive at every exec team meeting armed with my stats relevant to the business plan, not only about typical HR metrics. My team will have to provide me with these and be ready to explain their relevance to the business and the impact each one is having on the progress towards the 3-Year Plan."

I'm getting quite excited now, but Luisa shifts the focus. "Danielle, I'd like to know more about your team since their support will be vital in transforming the department. How would you describe the current dynamic?"

I smile. "They get along well. There's no rivalry between them because each performs well in their respective roles. The lines between their responsibilities are clear. If there's any tension at all, it's between Lauren, the Talent Manager, and Josh, our C&B Specialist. They're the team's newest members, ambitious and impatient. They're both eyeing the role of HR Director, though neither one has the broader HR experience that the role would call for.

"We work well together. They can all do what's needed without running to me whenever a problem arises, though I'm always there if they need me. Hmm. Now that I've said that out loud, I realize that *I want to know exactly what's going on in the department.*

"We have a daily briefing, so we all know what's happening. Sometimes, if there's an issue, we'll discuss the best solution, and they generally come up with that themselves. It takes 15-20 minutes maximum."

Sam and Luisa have been listening carefully as I talk. Sam now pushes me a little.

Sam summarizes. "From what you've told us, your team is perfectly capable of handling the day-to-day functioning of your department, but they're used to you being the decision maker, even for routine issues. How could you change that?"

"First," I reply, "I'll need to share the 3-Year Plan with them and focus on HR's role in achieving the company's objectives. Then, I'll ask them to work out what their area will need to contribute to the plan. Their responses will provide the basis for our HR plan.

"The most important thing will be for me to empower them to use their skills and experience and hold them accountable for the results. Once I've set the direction, my role will change from sole decision-maker to supporter and coach."

"So, how do you envision your team's role in contributing to the company's strategic direction?" Luisa asks.

"Well, giving details is hard because I don't have them yet. But let's say one aim is for the company to continue to grow. Talent acquisition will be critical, as will C&B's role in providing the data that ensures a realistic budget.

"If we want to increase sales," I continue, "it's about more than recruiting new people and rewarding them appropriately. It will need a considerable culture shift across every part of the operation because being customer-centric is something we haven't focused much on before.

"There'll be no point in recruiting new people if our attrition is high. Losing people comes at a high cost, so HR will be central to ensuring a positive employee experience and improving retention.

"As a result, everything we do will need to support achieving the business goals. It's my job to make sure the team is clear about that— not just what we're doing, but why it's important to the business."

Sam encourages me to get more specific. "How are you going to foster that culture of strategic thinking within your HR team?"

"It starts with me. I've got to get across to them that, starting now, we're shifting to a more future-facing approach. So, once I've got a handle on the strategic plan, we'll need to have a team meeting to go through it in detail, especially looking at next year's targets for the business, since we're already in Q4. They need to understand the 'why' as well as the 'what' if they're really going to buy into our goals."

"That sounds good," says Luisa. "Can you see any obstacles that could derail your plan to involve your team in creating their targets for next year?"

That's a good question. "One thing I need to focus on is the fact that the company is going through a cost-cutting phase. So I could encourage them to come up with ways to streamline our processes and find methods to optimize our costs."

Luisa interjects. "Do you think any savings you make could remove the threat of losing a team member?"

I shake my head. "Probably not, but that's not what I'll be aiming for. I doubt we could save the equivalent of a full salary. But it could be a way to get the team to link what we do with the company's overall priorities. Let's say the business needs to cut admin costs by 10% in order to grow. How are we going to play our part? Let's be innovative."

"Ah, I see," Sam says. "And are there other ways you can encourage them to think and act in a more future-facing way?"

"Yes, there are," I answer. "We need to create a strategic plan for HR so that I don't fall into the trap of just telling them to 'Be more strategic!' I'm going to have to take a coaching approach to change their mindset away from crossing tasks off their daily to-do list when they finish them to focusing on the things that'll move them closer to their long-term goals.

"As we co-create the HR Plan, I'll ask them to specify action steps and success measures for anything they come up with. That way, they'll play an integral part in shaping the role of HR for the next 1-3 years and be fully on board with the targets they're committing to.

"It'll be my role to get the COO to approve the plan and present it to the executive team so everyone knows where we're going. From then on, it will become the guiding light for all our activities."

Sam is thoughtful. "That's a great step, Danielle. Getting a plan in place with goals for the department. But is there a danger that the plan will get lost due to the demands of the daily HR tasks? How can you be sure that your team's activities are directly contributing to the achievement of organizational strategic objectives?"

I realize that this is the tricky part, and I need to think it through.

"We'll need to track our progress and ensure that it's the focus of all discussions and meetings. I'll share updates from the executive team with my team so we never lose sight of the broader strategy.

"I'll also be coaching the team to think ahead, anticipate any roadblocks, and support other departments in achieving their goals."

I've only answered half of his question and expect a follow-up. It comes from Luisa.

"Those things will be great in helping shift your team's mindset. But the daily work goes on. What are the critical elements you'll need to align within the team to support the overall direction of the business?"

"Hmm," I respond. "This is why I'll need to consider whether the current team structure is the most effective in the light of our changed priorities. I may have to go back to the drawing board. Imagine creating a new department solely to support the company's strategic plan. It may look completely different from the team that's grown organically over the years.

"I plan to request another team member, so I'll need to work out their role and how they will contribute to the plan. Where can they make the most significant impact on the business?

"At the same time—and this is still really uncomfortable for me to think about—I've been told to cut a team member. That may still happen, so I should be proactive in handling what I believe to be the worst-case scenario. Who would I lose, and how would the remaining team members handle their work?"

We all take a moment to consider the implications. I realize that being a future-facing team leader is not only about moving relentlessly toward a golden future. There may be obstacles ahead and hard decisions to be taken. *Being strategic is about anticipating situations, evaluating the options, and having the courage to stay on track.*

Luisa resumes the questions. "Danielle, you've mentioned how you're going to change the structure of your meetings. How are you going to tailor the way you speak to make sure your team understands and aligns with the organization's strategic direction?"

I need to think about this one. "One thing that springs to mind is the focus of our daily ops meetings. Each time I get an update, I've been focusing on: 'So what do we need to do about this today?' or 'Okay, job done, let's move on to the next task.'

"My questioning style needs to change to: *How will that activity affect the HR plan for this year?*' And I'll need to congratulate them on every step they make towards it. I guess I need to start speaking strategically.

"I can also share successes in other business areas with my team and celebrate our role in helping them achieve their goals. I'm sure they'll soon understand that everything we do has to align with the company's strategic direction."

I'm on a roll now. "And, oh, there are other things as well. It might seem a small thing, but it's another way of speaking strategically. We'll display our results and progress towards the company goals around the office for everyone to see, including visitors—make it clear that we are closely linked with the business and not just some satellite admin department that has no real connection with it. And that we are accountable for our results. We set goals—and achieve them!"

When I finally pause, out of breath but invigorated, Sam asks me to summarize where my thoughts have been leading me. "What steps will you take immediately to align your team with WMT's strategic direction?"

I lean forward in the chair. "Okay, first, to lead, I have to align myself and get to know our strategic direction! I have to internalize the fact that it is my role. Then, I have to get my team on board with WTM's goals for the next three years to develop an HR business plan. Of course, I'll guide that, but I want their input to play a big part. I want them to own it.

"I need to think about our priorities and speak in a way that makes it clear that HR is integral to achieving the company's overall business goals, not just today or even next year. Starting now—and inspired by you, Luisa—I'm changing how I organize my schedule and setting aside a short time daily to reflect on what and how I communicate with the team. I want to speak and act with authenticity.

"I have to work on two scenarios. The first, and the one I will work towards, is to make a compelling case for an additional team member to better support the business as it grows. I am ready to fight for that.

"The second is to consider what to do if I lose a team member, to look at the potential impact on our ability to contribute effectively. That will mean we won't be derailed if the worst happens."

Luisa nods. "These are major shifts in your approach, Danielle! How are you going to assess your progress and make necessary adjustments in the way you lead to ensure ongoing alignment?"

"To assess progress and keep the team aligned with the overall business? Well, if there's one thing we know how to do in HR, it's to track. I've implemented lots of tracking systems to streamline our processes and help us run efficiently. But we've not really been tracking progress towards specific targets. So that will change. We'll set up measurable targets to highlight progression towards our goals, which support the company's strategic business plan.

"Then, based on the results, if something isn't working, it will be my role to coach and guide the team and encourage them to come up with solutions that will get us back on the right road.

"In December, I'll ask them to set their objectives for the year ahead based on how each relates to the company business plan. And that, for the most part, will be how I'll evaluate their performance from now on."

Luisa smiles. "So, Danielle, that's plenty to work on! What would you say are the strengths and capabilities you already have that can aid you in leading your HR team strategically?"

"Well, I have a great relationship with my COO and the exec team, so I'm sure they'll be supportive once I share our new direction.

"The same goes for my team. They'll be as excited as I am about the new focus and take up the challenge to show what they're capable of. They'll appreciate that HR will be taking not exactly center-stage but can start to be seen as an essential player in the business.

"In terms of my strengths, I've got my MBA. I admit I've let what I learned while studying slide a little, and I've fallen into the trap of short-term thinking, concentrating on being seen as an efficient manager rather than the strategic team leader I know I can be. I'm impatient to change my approach and transition into an authentic VP role. I'm ready to lead my team towards the future. I'm up for a challenge—so bring it on, and I'll prove myself!"

"You've got this, Danielle," laughs Luisa, smiling at me.

Sam, as always, keeps us on track. How are you going to leverage the strengths of your team members to enhance strategic thinking and implementation in HR?"

"My Talent and Acquisition Manager, Lauren, is comfortable asking tough questions of managers and candidates. She can be invaluable in defining T&A targets for the HR plan and working with the business units to help determine their future needs—challenging them when needed and moving away from ad-hoc requests to a more structured approach.

"Josh, who looks after Comp and Bens, is a stats geek, so I see him as being able to create our goal trackers as we start. But more than that, he can work with Sara on the payroll costs as we grow and develop different scenarios to help the unit managers make the most effective use of their manpower budgets.

"I want to get him working on highlighting the cost of attrition, which some department heads need to be aware of. This will help focus the business on retaining talent and building a leadership pipeline for the future."

Luisa nods in agreement. "Those are both critical contributions to helping the business grow while keeping costs under control. What will you need to put in place to measure how closely your team is aligned with WMT's strategic direction? What kind of key performance indicators—KPIs—will highlight that?"

I have to think about this. I don't know the details of the strategic plan yet, but I can suggest a few ideas to support the company's growth.

"We already track time-to-fill for open positions and cost-per-hire. But we don't do much with the data we gather and haven't been sharing it with the executive team, who regard it as HR business. Communicating our progress towards reducing costs makes it *everyone's* business.

"As I've mentioned, retaining our best talent is critical, so we'll start tracking and sharing turnover rates, especially among high-performing and high-potential employees. Reducing the turnover rate indicates how successfully we contribute, whether by selecting the right people, making sure compensation stays in line with the market, training and coaching their leaders, or creating engagement initiatives that help brand us as an employer of choice.

"Another area we haven't tracked so far is diversity and inclusion. The executive team made a commitment a couple of years back. Still, we need to measure the effectiveness of DEI initiatives through metrics such as representation of underrepresented groups, employee satisfaction with our diversity programs, and promotion rates among diverse employees.

"As we continue to grow, I'll need to ensure that we're constantly improving the employee experience and enhancing our employer brand. So I want to set a target to boost our eNPS—the Employee Net Promoter Score—by next year. I'll give my team the task of proposing HR initiatives in their area to help us achieve that. However, engagement isn't only an HR issue, so I'll ask them to contact the department heads to develop initiatives. Once we've created the overall plan, I'll request the CEO to champion company-wide programs and each exec team member to drive the initiatives in their department, with my team's support."

Sam glances at his phone since my time is almost up.

But he has one last question for me. "The same question I asked Luisa. *What if you do nothing?* What if you go back to the office, stay busy with day-to-day issues, and never find time to be a strategic leader for your team?"

I laugh. "If that happens, I'd better get used to losing one of my team members and trying to do the same old work, with fewer resources. Their work will have to be allocated to the others, who won't be impressed. They may look for opportunities outside the company. I'll lose credibility as a leader, and I'll probably end up taking on more of the mundane workload.

"The rest of the business will continue to treat HR as a reactive department that carries out instructions and processes paperwork. I'll feel like I wasted all those years studying, and I certainly won't get any closer to achieving my long-term CHRO ambition. It would be really, um...." I trail off, my energy fading.

Enough! I stop. "Sorry, I'm losing brain power." I raise my eyes and smile at my two Socratic guides. *"I'm not going to let any of that happen.*

"Guys, I can't thank you enough for helping me start organizing my ideas and finding my direction.

"Now, I'm going to step up and do what it takes to become a future-focused team leader who thinks, speaks, and acts strategically. By leveraging my team's capabilities, HR will become a driver of the company's success. I'll ensure that my department is allocated the resources it needs—an investment, not a cost."

Danielle and Sam smile broadly but say nothing. And so my segment of the meeting is over. *I've come a long way in a short time.*

I realize that I've been avoiding the real challenges of leading a team strategically. I've now thought through some of the actions I can take to transition from a reactive to a more future-focused approach to the challenges ahead. I see how a few simple, practical actions can impact my effectiveness as a team leader. And it all starts with my understanding of the company's strategic business plan.

I'm grateful that the Socratic method has guided me and provided a space to clarify my thinking. Sam's and Luisa's questioning has brought me valuable insights. I feel empowered to approach business challenges by leading my team to think, speak, and act in ways that address the future. I'm filled with the confidence and energy I'd been in danger of losing.

But most of all right now, I can't wait to get back to work and start the journey that will transform my department team and enable us to contribute to my company's long-term growth and success.

Now, I'm excited to see where Sam's dialogue will lead us—and the insights it will bring.

While we take a quick break, I make the most of the opportunity to jot down my thoughts.

Preparing For Change: Thinking Strategically

- ✓ Review the company's business plan. Get a handle on the priorities and statistics to inform discussions with the COO and my peers
- ✓ Consider the implications of losing a team member, the benefits of strengthening the team
- ✓ Decide which of my routine tasks I can delegate to my team
- ✓ Research coaching styles and maybe get some training to polish my skills

Making The Transition: Speaking Strategically

- ✓ Schedule team company plan in detail
- ✓ Use future-facing questions to focus the team
- ✓ Empower them to use their skills and experience and make them accountable for results
- ✓ Get team to set their objectives for the year ahead and agree on KPIs
- ✓ Display our results and progress towards goals

Embedding The Change: Acting Strategically

- ✓ Create a strategic HR Plan with input from the team and assign goals to each individual
- ✓ Create a new team structure and make my case to the COO
- ✓ Create a cost optimization plan
- ✓ Track and publish HR KPIs
- ✓ Coach my team as required

Reflections for the Reader

1. THINK

✓ How well do I know the details of my company's strategic business plan? Am I able to use it to inform my plan for HR?

✓ How willing am I to face harsh realities? Do I grapple with them to find the best solution, or do I prefer to 'wait and see,' hoping that the worst never happens?

✓ Do my team members view me as a leader who has a vision of where we're heading? Or as a boss who gives them instructions and monitors their work?

2. SPEAK

✓ How do I speak to my team when sharing good news? What about when sharing difficult news?

✓ How effective am I as a facilitator? How comfortable? Do my facilitation skills need refreshing or upgrading?

✓ How do I communicate HR's plans and progress to the wider company? Can everyone see how HR is contributing?

3. ACT

✓ What has changed in the company since I created the HR plan? Has the plan been updated to reflect any changes?

✓ Do my KPIs (key performance indicators) reflect the current business situation? Do my team's?

CHAPTER

5

NAVIGATING THE UNKNOWN

In the midst of chaos, there is also opportunity.

— *Sun Tzu, The Art of War*

Sam takes his turn at Strategic Thinking

Although this is our first session together, I'm impressed by how much the technique of Socratic inquiry has helped Luisa and Danielle open up, get straight to the heart of their most pressing issue, and work out a way forward.

Now, it's my turn in the hot seat, and I'm ready.

Luisa eases us gently into the conversation. "Before we start, Sam, would you mind giving us an overview of your role at WAT, We Automate Things?"

"Of course," I respond confidently and with a big smile. *After all, I'm the last one to present my case study, so I was lucky to get the benefit of all the earlier feedback.* I remember all my well-studied presentation skills as I turn to my audience of two and make strong eye contact.

"I was hired as the company's first CHRO just one month ago. At my interviews, they didn't present a lot of detail in terms of priorities, but they did place a lot of emphasis on my need to be strategic since the company has grown so fast and wants to continue on that trajectory."

"I think I heard about WAT," says Danielle. "Perhaps you could start by giving us a little background on the company. What has made it grow so quickly?"

"Yes, sure. WAT was founded less than five years ago by our current CEO. He's an entrepreneur who, at the age of 28, together with a few friends, developed some game-changing tech. There's no doubt that it's brilliant. And he enjoys being in the spotlight. You've probably even seen him on the cover of various business magazines as a rising star—or on podcasts being interviewed about his opinions on just about everything."

The women nod, glance at each other, and then turn their eyes back to me.

"So, the company started with a team of four and just grew to where it is today. My boss has already turned down offers from the big players who are ready to buy his tech and make him a billionaire overnight. Instead, he's funded our growth by attracting investors eager to be part of an exciting story. Recently, I've heard rumors that we're getting ready to float on the NY Stock Exchange, though nothing has been said publicly, and I have no idea whether that's true or not.

"Right now, we have over 1,300 employees. The business has grown kind of haphazardly, according to whatever was needed at the time. The place has incredible energy, and people are almost fanatically committed to the founder and the company, which is usually an asset. But—"

Luisa interrupts with a grin. "I knew there would be a 'but'!" she chuckles.

I laugh and continue, "Yes, the 'but' is that every department seems to be working almost independently. They're like rival kingdoms at war. There's such competition between them—even up to the director level. It reminds me of *Game of Thrones.*"

Danielle interjects. "How is this wild culture affecting performance and business results?"

"Good question, Danielle," I say. "Until now, WAT has been riding high on a wave of success. But there's growing concern that rivals are snapping at our heels, and everyone is so busy infighting that no one seems to notice. I've never seen that in any of my previous roles—and certainly never in the military. Everything is so unclear that priorities seem to change according to who I speak to.

"And the boss is always on the move. There's very little structured communication, though he randomly posts his thoughts on our Discord server for everyone to discuss. Naturally, he gravitates towards the R&D team because innovation is, as he says, 'the lifeblood of the business.' When he comes up with an idea, he tells the person who happens to be next to him then—and the chances are, they'll go off and do it! But by that time, he'll have moved on to something else."

Danielle probes further. "Wow, that's fascinating! But I can see how that environment could be a real challenge. How has your first month gone?"

"It hasn't. That's the problem. I feel like I've been parachuted into unfamiliar terrain without a compass. I'm lost, and I don't know how to start finding a way out. I was brought in to be a 'World-Class' CHRO, but I'm beginning to lose all confidence in my ability and feel like I'm just not up to the role." My face falls as I reveal my low morale.

"But it's not as if I arrived at the company without any plan at all. For the first month, I set three priorities, which the CEO and I discussed when he called to welcome me on board.

"First, I was planning a listening tour to get to know the executive team and other key players. I wanted to take my time to understand the business and hear from people at every level about how it was going. Second, I was to get to know my HR team, and learn how they've been working and where they saw our priorities. The Third was to conduct a listening tour to understand the current culture and determine the next steps.

"My first port of call was the CEO's office. But he's been away most of that time, so I've barely been able to see him. I've had meetings with the other directors to better understand the business, our strengths, and our challenges. How they see the future. And that has helped me! But only to see how little alignment there is between the leaders. I don't see how to move forward without an overriding goal to pull us all together.

"For example, I have to create next year's budget. *But without a plan, how can I start to know where to target our financial resources?*"

Luisa asks, "Can't you get the support you need from the CFO?"

I shrug. "Up to a point, yes. But one of the most common complaints about HR leaders is that they're disconnected from the financial realities of the business. So the last thing I want to do is delegate my responsibilities to Finance, or to make a proposal that's not clear about the impact that HR will have on the company's profit and loss."

"I see your dilemma," Danielle says with empathy.

"I got this job because I assured them I was up for the challenge. And the danger of that is: The longer I procrastinate, the more credibility I lose with the CEO and my peers.

"They say that in any new role, you only have three months to create your personal brand. One month in, and I've made zero progress on the one concrete thing I've been asked to do. I've achieved nothing that would earn me respect and prove I belong on the exec team of WAT." *I'm probably looking pretty defeated at the moment.*

"What makes you think that, Sam?" asks Luisa with concern.

"Well, I'm the new kid on the block. I'm new to the company, and this is my first CHRO role. My peers seem to think my role here is just to support them. So, for example, I wasn't asked to be part of the task force working on the company budget. The CFO just 'instructed' me to create the company's HR budget. But I'm not his subordinate! We're peers on the organizational chart."

Luisa clearly wants to explore this further. "But surely, every company needs a budget as a framework. It's fundamental. How could you put together something that has value to the business?"

I nod. "Well, yes, I could approach it in a couple of ways. I could base a plan on previous budgets, adjusting them according to growth forecasts or spending constraints. But that would only be taking account of the past, not the future. And because it won't be based on the company's priorities, how will I know where best to allocate resources? I'm also responsible for monitoring the HR budget over the year. How will it make me more credible if my forecasts are wildly out of line with what the business needs?" I sigh in exasperation.

Luisa gives me an affirming smile. "You're right, Sam. But the HR budget doesn't just affect HR—it impacts the whole company. So how can you get the support you need?"

Grateful for her support, I offer, thoughtfully: "I could ask each department for their ideas about what line items in the HR budget they'll need in the year ahead. But then, of course, the results will depend on whose voice is the loudest. There's nothing strategic about it, because I'm not clear about the company's goals for the coming year, and neither are my peers. So how will I be able to prioritize?"

My frustration comes through in my facial expression and body language. It's clear that none of us are satisfied with the solutions so far.

Danielle takes a turn. "Do you have any other sources of information?"

"Yes, some," I respond. "I've already done a lot of research into business trends. I've looked at how our industry is moving and how much it's predicted to grow over the next decade. I've also studied broad HR trends, like the tightening talent market, how to retain Gen Z employees, and new thinking around fair compensation models— oh, and also about the opportunities to use AI for training and development, cutting costs, and improving outcomes."

Luisa's eyes widen. "Sounds like you've got plenty to go on."

We all sit silently for a few moments as we consider my dilemma.

Danielle breaks our pensiveness and returns to what I said earlier. "Sam, what was it that made you believe you were up to the challenge in the first place? What gave you the confidence to go for this role?"

I think about it for a few moments before responding. "With fifteen years of active military service under my belt, I understand the need to take action to reach a goal. But, to do that, there needs to be a chain of command. It's the responsibility of the commander to communicate what the mission is and what the goal is that you are all moving towards. From there, you need to know what resources you have available. And you need to know that the people you'll be relying on are capable and have your back, and they all have the same goal as you. You know?"

Luisa and Danielle nod in agreement. "Yeah, absolutely," Luisa says.

I continue, now a little didactic as if I'm giving a formal presentation. I pull out a piece of paper and begin to write a list. "With those four things in place," I say as I write and then speak the following:

1. *Command structure*
2. *Clear communication of the mission or goal*
3. *Adequate resources or tools*
4. *A capable team with the same goal*

"...you're ready to move forward and achieve a victory."

"Yes," Luisa says.

Danielle probes further. "And what about your experience in business after leaving the military? Have you been able to leverage that expertise?"

I feel my confidence rising as I explain. "In essence, yes. In other companies, there was always a strategic business plan in place. The overall aims and steps to achieve them were clear. Each department, including HR, created plans to support that. So, the overall plan cascaded down through the business, and everyone knew the part they had to play.

"Once I knew what I had to achieve, those higher up in the organization could leave the details and the tactics to me. I'd make sure I had sufficient resources—and use them efficiently—so that my team and I would progress in alignment toward the goal.

"You know, I never failed to hit a target I set for myself or my team." I beam with self-satisfaction. "That earned me my reputation for being the guy you could trust to *deliver and get things done*. That's what helped me climb the HR career ladder faster than most," I say proudly. Then the frustration breaks through again. "But now I feel like I've hit a brick wall. I just don't know where to go next."

Luisa speaks up. "That's never a good feeling. Are you able to identify your most pressing challenge? The one that, if you overcome it, will help you shatter that brick wall?"

I nod. "On the surface, that's easy. It's the budget that's got me stuck. Without an overall business plan that defines the company goals for the next few years, how can I create and align an HR budget? I can't get past this." I sigh audibly.

We all pause and think. Then, out of nowhere, it hits me: that lightbulb moment I've been waiting for.

"Just a minute. Actually, no, that's not my most pressing challenge! I've just realized: The HR budget is important, yes—*but it's not the mission I've been brought in to achieve.*"

I pull out another piece of paper and write. *"My mission as CHRO is to help create an organization that will enable the company to grow and be sustainable into the future."*

I show the paper to my colleagues with renewed energy. "So, for now, I can get my HR management team started on an outline budget and ensure that Finance will at least have some ballpark figures to work with."

Now that I'm thinking strategically, as the conference speaker promised, I can see my goal more clearly.

Danielle takes it further. "Okay, so you've realized that you were getting blocked by just one aspect of your overall role, and now you're getting to the heart of the issue. Good progress forward, Sam! But let me ask you. Again, with your military background, how can you apply your skills to achieve the mission you've just defined?"

I'm thinking more clearly now, and I respond. "To help create an organization that will enable the company to grow and be sustainable into the future, I'll still need four things." I start to write them on another sheet of paper. I need a whiteboard! "First, I need to clarify the company's overall aim—what do we want to achieve?

"Then, I need to ensure that the aim is communicated clearly to every stakeholder.

"Third, I'll need to make sure we have the resources required to achieve the aim—the right people, the right capabilities, and the right rewards." I'm furiously scribbling my notes on the paper as I speak.

"And fourth, I'll need to provide the leadership to keep everyone on the right track and moving forwards." I set down the pen and turn to Luisa and Danielle with a glow of satisfaction in my eyes.

Luisa takes the reins. "Now that you're thinking this through, Sam, maybe it will help if we look at each of those four things in turn?"

"Good idea!" Danielle chimes in.

Luisa picks up the paper and reads the first point. "First, you say you'll need to clarify the overall aim of the company. How are you going to do that?"

I jump in. "I have to get the CEO on board. The problem is, he regards HR as something necessary but not really interesting. I can't just go to him and talk about why a 3- or 5-year plan is a good idea. He thrives on being agile, but I need to help him see how the lack of a coherent strategy is damaging to the company's growth prospects. Investors and shareholders want to know where we're going, and that can't change from one day to the next—it will make them nervous about how we're protecting their investment. I'm going to need to speak strategically and show him what the future may look like."

Danielle responds, "It sounds as if you might have a hard time pinning him down so he'll focus on creating a plan. How will you deal with that?"

I grimace. "Yeah, you're right. I need his help. But I can't go in there looking weak and hesitant. I've been hired with a mission, and I need to let the commander-in-chief understand the terrain and focus his attention on the risks of not having a strategy to beat the competition. I'll need to be armed with facts and data and speak in a way that will grab his attention. I'll convince him by laying out the best-case and worst-case scenarios.

"So, to prepare, I'll research our competitors and look at the fate of other businesses that have shot from zero to 100 in a short time. How did it work out for them? How many shooting stars ended up crashing and burning? How did the ones who made it, and are still successful today, do that? How did they evolve?

"That should make it clear to him that a plan will not hold us back but instead will guide us toward the future we want. I want him to see that he needs to get his troops lined up and communicate clearly to them. After that, he can step back and let them do what's needed."

"So what exactly will you be convincing him to do, Sam?" Luisa wants me to clarify. *Maybe I'm using too many military analogies.*

I step up to the plate. "I'll be convincing him to lead a strategic planning process and to create a business plan that will clarify his vision and define our goals for the next 1, 3, or 5 years. The company will use it to guide all our decisions and efforts. The strategic plan will serve as the roadmap that brings everyone together and turns his vision into reality! It has to start with him, then cascade through the business, so that each director, every team leader, and every individual contributor knows their role in supporting the achievement of that vision."

"And your role?" Danielle asks.

"In the short term, it's clear. I will be getting this process underway and driving the creation of the CEO-led plan. Whether I suggest bringing in a consultancy with experience in helping businesses at our growth stage—or decide to lead the process myself—I'm not sure yet.

"Once that's done, I also want to work with the CEO to define his role as we go forward. He has terrific charisma and has built the company's profile in the media, creating a great buzz. So I'll encourage him to work with the External Comms team and focus on articulating his plans for the business. Meanwhile, he has a team of experienced and talented directors who can operate the business, so he doesn't need to focus on the details as he has done in the past."

Danielle nods enthusiastically and brings me back to my four points. "So, Sam, you're going to clarify the role of the overall commander. You also mentioned the need for clear communication. How will you encourage that?"

"Yes, good question, thanks!" I respond. "A new communications strategy will be an integral part of the plan. First, each department head will need to cascade the new plan and priorities throughout the organization. Every employee will need to set goals, as soon as possible, that contribute to their section's, their department's, and the company's goals.

"We'll need new ways to track progress and highlight achievements, and HR will need to recommend new ways of rewarding success." I pause and take a breath. "So, those are just my initial ideas—I don't have a firm plan in place yet. I'll need to think all this through in more detail."

"Great!" Luisa says, moving me along to the next issue. "Now, with a clear goal, a structure, and lines of communication in place, the next thing you said you'd need to win a battle is to have the resources or tools. How would you apply this to your situation?"

I'm ready for her. "Well, by this, I mean: Do we have the 'hardware' we need? Yes. From what I've seen and heard, that's not an issue. But how do we make sure we have the talent we're going to need as we grow? How do we make sure they have the right capabilities as the company evolves?

"And here is where the financial resources will play a critical role. To ensure that the business has what it needs, I need to create a strategic HR plan for the business and back it up with a breakdown of cost and the benefits of each action step I'm proposing."

"Which brings us nicely back to the budget," says Luisa with a smile.

"And what resources will you need to create that HR plan?" asks Danielle.

"This is where I'll need full involvement and support from my peers. I can't sit in a room on my own or with my HR team and write this plan. While it will be 'owned' and driven by HR, it has to reflect the needs of the overall company. Each department has to see how it will contribute to their success.

"So, I have to go to the department heads and listen to what they tell me about the HR support they're going to need in the future to help them achieve the company goals. I'll guide and advise them, making sure our priorities align with our aims for growth in future. From that point, it will become my responsibility as CHRO to monitor our progress towards achieving it."

"Which I guess, again, leads us nicely back to the budget!" Luisa chuckles. We all smile.

But I have a few minutes left, so Luisa continues the questioning. "Can you identify potential allies or mentors within your organization who could guide you in this strategic endeavor?"

"Yes," I say with confidence. "It's time I reached out to the CFO. He's a powerful voice in the company, and I need to get him on my side. So far, we've had general discussions and touched on HR issues in his department. He sees HR as a cost but not a business asset. But if I share my thinking on how we need to prepare for the future, he could be a strong ally.

"Also, there's the VP of R&D. When we spoke, he was concerned about how we could continue to develop groundbreaking new products with the current turnover of engineering talent. I didn't really have an answer for him at the time. Now I do. It's not just his problem—or HR's problem. We all need to work together to address this challenge, because without the talent to reinvent our offerings, the company will stagnate."

Danielle glances at her phone and indicates that my time is nearly up. "So, Sam, I feel we've come a long way in this discussion. Will it help you to summarize your journey?"

I take a deep breath. "Let me think. At the start of our conversation, I was blocked, stuck in the past, and only thinking about what was lacking in my new role—a plan for the company, any support, and my confidence.

"My thinking has changed, and now I can see a way forward. In essence, the company has no updated strategic plan, which is an issue for the whole business, as no one's priorities are clear. Supported by relevant information, I need to lead the creation of a future-facing, CEO-driven plan that will unite us.

"From there, armed with insight from across the company, I will be in a solid position to create and drive forward a strategic plan for HR that's closely aligned with the company's future goals. Based on this, I'll produce a budget aligned with organizational needs."

That's it. Wow. Using the Think-Speak-Act model, I've come a long way in such a short time. I share my thoughts. "You know, by shifting my mindset to think more strategically, it's so clear that I need to stop focusing on what is lacking and, instead, consider what we need for the future.

"In the past, I've always led by following a clear direction and structured plan. Now, I need to shift my mindset and grow in leading the creation and implementation of a strategic plan. I know my goals, and now I need to speak strategically with the CEO and my peers.

"In the CEO's case, it's about speaking truth to power so that he can see clearly how aligning everyone will help us progress to growth and a sustainable future.

"From there, acting strategically and facilitating the creation of a company-wide strategic plan and an HR plan to support that will be the natural outcomes."

All three of us smile. I continue, "Well, all I can say is thank you for the most productive fifteen minutes I've had since I joined WAT!"

Meeting over, we all head off in different directions to think over what we've discussed today. Our next meeting will be in three weeks, so I'm looking forward to discovering how much of what we've discussed turns into reality. *I'm expecting things at WAT to start looking very different very soon.*

Reflections for the Reader

1. THINK

- ✓ What do I think are the characteristics of a "world-class" CHRO?
- ✓ In the absence of a strategic plan, what are the steps I would take to define my priorities?
- ✓ How agile is my thinking? How capable am I at overcoming obstacles and creating inventive solutions to business challenges?

2. SPEAK

- ✓ How confident am I in speaking truth to power?
- ✓ What steps do I take to maintain rapport and credibility when bringing up new ideas to initiate change?

3. ACT

- ✓ Once I've decided on a course of action, do I hesitate to put it into action? What is my approach to action that involves a degree of risk?
- ✓ How do I differentiate my role as an HR leader from my role as an executive leader within the organization? In what ways do these roles complement each other in driving strategic outcomes?

CHAPTER

6

THE ASPIRING STRATEGIST

Believe you can and you're halfway there.

— *Theodore Roosevelt*

Luisa begins to turn her good intentions into reality

Arriving back at the office, I settle down at my desk, excited at the journey I've been on with Danielle and Sam. I'm ready to face the future, so let the transformation begin!

Within two minutes, Rob, my HR Specialist, interrupts my reverie before I've even had a chance to enjoy it. An urgent issue has arisen regarding two employees in a business unit about 30 minutes' drive from the office. Their manager is at wit's end, others are getting involved, work has stopped, it could even turn violent—and he doesn't know how to handle it. How soon can I get there?

I know that this particular manager has recently been promoted. I can almost feel the old Luisa rising from her chair and grabbing her coat. But the new Luisa resists the urge.

"Rob, you've handled employee conflicts before now. How would you help the manager to calm things down?"

He tells me.

"And what would you suggest they do to ensure that there's no repeat of the situation?"

He tells me.

"Sounds like a good plan. So, I'm sure you can deal with it. Just follow up with the manager to make sure he's confident that it's resolved and that he knows how to deal with it if it happens again."

Off he goes, although reluctantly. Now, I can settle down and start thinking strategically. The first step is to block my calendar for 90 minutes daily. That will work best at the end of the day so I can reflect on what's happened and prepare for the future.

No sooner have I done that than I get a call from Sophie, the exec assistant I share with the CEO. "Hey, Luisa, the boss wants to know if you have time for a catch up—about recruitment, I think."

The old Luisa is ready to say, "Of course, what time?"

The new Luisa says, "Sure, but let me call him so I know exactly what he needs from me and can be sure I have the relevant information when I see him. That way, we'll make the best use of our time."

I call him, and although he's surprised at my request, when I explain that I would also like to understand more about his business priorities for the coming year to help me prepare for the planning meeting, we agree on a time the next day that will work for both of us.

For the third time, I try to settle down to start being strategic—and I can't pretend that it all goes smoothly.

People constantly drop in to see me, to ask for advice, to complain, or just because they're taking a break from their work and feel like chatting.

I realize that changing how I'm perceived in the company will take some time. Everyone trusts me, and I don't want to lose my reputation for being authentic by switching abruptly from the "old Luisa" to a "new Luisa."

If I change my behavior overnight, I'm going to alienate the very people who support me. They might take it personally, which is the last thing I want. As I consider this, I realize that, for the most part, I've enjoyed my reputation as always being approachable, trustworthy, and more of a friend than a leader in the business.

I reflect and ask myself: "Is this new, strategic way of being really me? Would I be happier if I let things go on just like before? Am I trying to become someone that, deep down, I'm not?"

But I know that things around me are about to change dramatically. Being passive and doing nothing is not an option. The key will be to remain faithful to my authentic self and change my approach so that I'm working in the most effective way to help sustain and grow the business—all while still being Luisa.

Day One

Finally, the moment comes. It's time for the first of my daily strategic sessions, and I keep my promise to myself. For the next three weeks, I will dedicate this part of the day to preparing for that critical meeting.

I start clarifying my thoughts by creating a list, each point under one of three headings: think, speak, act. This ensures that I'm addressing each aspect of **being strategic**.

At this point, it's more of a brainstorm than a comprehensive plan. *I may change it entirely after I dive in, but at least it's what I need to get started.*

The first draft looks like this.

Before the Meeting: Think Strategically

- ✓ Prepare questions for each Department Head in the planning meeting
- ✓ Get curious. Research the market and the competition, and then ask future-facing questions.
- ✓ Reach out to the strategy consultant to help me prep for the meeting
- ✓ What are the cultural implications of sales team integration?
- ✓ Develop options for compensation design for the sales team.

During the Meeting: Speak Strategically

- ✓ Engage Department Heads in strategic discussions: Ask forward-facing questions
- ✓ Actively participate in the discussion and analysis
- ✓ Facilitate collaborative discussions arising from my presentation

After the Meeting: Act Strategically

- ✓ Collate all their needs and develop a vision for HR's role in the next 3 years
- ✓ Following the meeting: Create steps to achieve the vision for HR's Role
- ✓ Facilitate collaborative discussions between different parts of the business

It feels good to organize my thoughts. Next, I start to flesh out each point so I can decide what steps to take for each one.

Starting with my intention to **think** strategically, I add details to each bullet point. I start with an easy step, but it's one that will commit me to action.

Think Strategically

Goal 1: Engage my CEO and Department Heads in strategic discussions

Action Items:

- ✓ Schedule meetings, starting next week – first, I want to give myself a few days to research and prepare for the meetings.
- ✓ Ask Sophie to organize the schedule and block out my calendar.

Although scheduling the meetings is by no means the full story, I decide that I've completed what I needed to do today. I place a check mark next to this bullet. *Feels good!*

Next, I consider exactly what I'll need to do to ensure that these meetings have a strategic focus. I state an aim before I list the steps.

Goal 2: Get curious. Research the market and the competition and ask strategic questions.

Q: What's my aim here?

A: To understand big-picture impacts and not necessarily be a subject-matter expert. To understand the business well enough to ask idea-generating/potential impact/unintended-consequence questions (i.e., to be able to address future priorities and challenges in the planning meeting).

Action Items

Step 1: Reach out to my CEO. There's only one aim here. I want to understand his top three business priorities for the year ahead: why each one is so important and which is giving him the most concern.

Step 2: Reach out to my peers inside WFT: meetings already confirmed.

Step 3: Reach out to peers outside WFT: Post a request on our local HR Groups networking page and ask whether there's anyone who's been part of the leadership team when their company goes through a major expansion or change of direction.

Step 4: Research online to learn more about the current state of the market in the domestic retail appliance sector.

Other Notes

Our current VP of Sales should have plenty of background information, growth forecasts, sales targets, etc., and I'm meeting him next week.

And surely the Strategy Consultant will have valuable data—and I'll add that to the list of questions I'm preparing for her if she agrees to meet. (If she can't make it, I'll email my list to her.)

> I can also search LinkedIn for some practical ideas. It's packed with short articles that could get me focused on how we can address this challenge in a way that meets the needs of existing employees as well as new recruits.

The more I work on elaborating each action item, the easier it's becoming to come up with ideas that will help me prepare for the future. I continue.

Goal 3: Develop options for compensation design for the sales team

Aim: Use data to propose an approach to their compensation that will attract and retain the best talent while generating the target ROI.

Action Items

- ✓ WFT works with a number of recruiters who help us source talent at all levels. I'm going to leverage those relationships and ask them to provide their latest data on Sales team compensation.

- ✓ Then, a) I can share it with the Finance Director, who's likely already working on the budget for the expansion, and b) in the strategic planning, I can propose some broad-brush compensation approaches that we as a team could agree on.

- ✓ Do we want to match the market salary level, or slightly underpay and focus on a generous bonus model? Once I have the data, I'll be able to propose what I see as the most effective approach and counter any challenges with facts instead of vague feelings.

I consider all the conversations I'm committing to over the next three weeks and realize just how profoundly this mini-brainstorm of my priorities is going to transform the way I work.

That's enough for one day! I can't believe the shift in my thinking since this morning. I reread my list of aims and steps and am impressed with my clear direction.

On the second day of my daily "Strategic 90" sessions, I start by focusing on how I'm going to **speak** more strategically in preparation for and during the planning meeting.

Think Strategically

Step One: Communicate my Vision for HR's Role

✓ I'll define this after my meetings with the CEO and my peers. I will also use what I've learned from my HR peers in the local network, as well as any resources I've found or the consultant has shared with me, to inform my vision.

✓ I will prepare a presentation to articulate a clear vision for HR's strategic contribution to the business over the next 1-3 years, including the retail expansion and the addition of a sales team.

✓ I will make it clear that our priorities extend beyond traditional HR functions, and our mission is to support the company's growth and sales objectives.

Step Two: Facilitate Collaborative Discussions

✓ Over the next two weeks, I'll be encouraging department heads (not only the VP of Sales) to share their thoughts on aligning the expansion and sales with departmental objectives. I'll go into each meeting with a list of strategic, future-facing questions to ensure that the discussion stays on track.

✓ I'll request the meeting agenda from the strategy consultant and propose where I could present the HR vision and lead a discussion that transcends immediate HR impacts.

I'm surprised that being "strategic" isn't as abstract as I'd previously thought. The "thinking" and "speaking" steps I've listed all involve clear, practical actions that, one by one, should lead me to create a new, future-facing direction for HR—one that is intimately connected with the business. This realization leads me to consider the likely outcomes for HR after the meeting and some of the key areas I'd be focusing on.

Key Strategic Actions after the Planning Meeting

Priority One: Aligning HR Initiatives with Company Goals

✓ Given the priorities that will be agreed upon in the meeting, I'll need to review the structure of the current HR function and consider whether the headcount and budget we're allocated is fit for purpose. I'm already realizing that we'll need more resources, so I'll prepare my case. Me plus one full-time and one half-time employee won't be enough to deliver what's needed to drive the expansion and cultural shift. Then, after the meeting, I need to analyze in more detail and specify exactly the level of expertise I'll need to bring in.

✓ I'll also need to revisit our talent acquisition strategies to support the evolving organizational structure, including the integration of a sales team. Will we bring a recruiter onto the team or use outside consultants?

✓ I'll need to ensure that HR policies are updated to align with the broader company goals, especially considering the cultural shift from repair-only to sales and service.

✓ Working with my peers, I'll need to drive the development of a company-wide training and development plan, including programs to prepare employees—especially the new sales team—for their roles.

Priority Two: Creating a Strategic HR Roadmap

✓ I need to develop a roadmap that clearly outlines HR's contributions to the retail expansion and the addition of a sales team.

✓ I need to include specific initiatives, timelines, and anticipated outcomes for both departments and make clear where additional resources will be required to achieve it.

✓ I also need to consider the level of "ownership" that the respective departments (Retail & Sales) will have for rolling out these initiatives—and get the Heads on board before I finalize anything.

✓ I'm going to draft a roadmap for my own use before the planning meeting and present a high-level version at the meeting. I'll finalize it based on the priorities the team agrees on.

✓ In the meeting, I'm going to commit to sharing the roadmap within three days of the planning meeting to emphasize HR's commitment to driving strategic change.

So, these are the steps to transform the perception of HR as a passive administrative function into one capable of making a powerful strategic impact on the future of the company.

And yes, when I follow the Think-Act-Speak model, ***being strategic*** comes naturally and authentically.

Now, I'm totally excited as the meeting approaches. I can't wait for my next meeting with Sam and Danielle so I can share my success with my two guides!

Reflections for the Reader

1. THINK

- ✓ How much time do I allocate for planning? For reflection?
- ✓ How many of my regular tasks could I delegate? Are there any that are no longer productive that I could drop?
- ✓ How do I handle visitors who "drop in" for impromptu meetings? Are they a valuable use of my time?
- ✓ How much do I know about our competitors or about consumer trends in our industry?
- ✓ How often do I consider the culture of my organization and the role of HR in shaping it?

2. SPEAK

- ✓ Am I an active participant in meetings? How well am I prepared with facts and questions?
- ✓ How proactive am I in engaging my peers in strategic discussions? Do I ask probing questions to help explore issues and identify multiple solutions?
- ✓ How well do I communicate my vision of HR's role? (to my team, to my peers, across the company)

3. ACT

- ✓ How often do I update HR policies and programs to ensure that they still align with the strategic direction of the business?
- ✓ How proactive am I in proposing and creating new initiatives aligned with the strategic direction of the business?

CHAPTER

7

THE PROPOSAL

*Do not go where the path may lead; go
instead where there is no path and leave
a trail.*

— *Ralph Waldo Emerson*

**Danielle continues her journey towards becoming a strategic
team leader**

After meeting with Luisa and Sam, I spent last evening with
my mind racing, distracted. My partner wanted to talk about
our upcoming vacation. My mom called me to catch up and,
inevitably, tell me about the daughter of one of her friends who had
just become engaged, got married, had a baby—or, who knows, gone
to Mars! But my thoughts were elsewhere, and I couldn't wait to get
to my desk this morning.

I get to the office before anyone else arrives. I grab a coffee, close the
door, and take a deep breath. *How do I get started thinking, speaking,
and acting strategically?* I open my notebook and start to organize
my thoughts with a very basic to-do list.

1. **Think strategically:** Review company strategic plan (in detail).
2. **Speak strategically:** Meet with the COO and get his support for an HR Strategic Plan aligned with the company plan. Set a deadline.
3. **Speak strategically:** Share the company plan with my team and coach the mindset for thinking about how HR contributes now and in the future.
4. **Think strategically:** Co-create the HR plan with input from my team, making sure to optimize costs in line with the 10% requirement.
5. **Speak strategically:** Present the HR plan to the COO.
6. **Think strategically:** Review current team roles in light of the proposed HR plan.
7. **Get approval by COO** (fingers crossed!)
8. **Speak strategically:** Present the HR Plan to the CEO & exec team.
9. **Act strategically:** Implement the HR Strategic Plan.

It's not the most comprehensive outline, perhaps, but at least it'll get me started.

I book a meeting time on the COO's calendar.

Next, I block time on my calendar to start my deep dive into the company's strategic plan.

When my team arrives, I briefly explain to them what I'm working on and encourage them to handle the operations as smoothly as they always do.

Now, back to studying the strategic plan. Before I start, I reflect on the purpose of a strategic plan. Why do we even have one, and what was the exec team trying to achieve when they created it?

Then I remember something about this from my MBA course, so I pull up my old class notes on my tablet for some review on theory. Luckily, the notes are impeccably organized (because I'm that kind of person!), and I find what I'm looking for almost immediately.

Why Create a Three-Year Strategic Business Plan?

The strategic business plan will serve as a roadmap, outlining a company's objectives, goals, and strategies for achieving sustainable growth and success over the next three years. The purpose of the plan includes:

1. **Direction and focus:** The plan provides clarity on the company's direction and its medium-term goals. By defining specific goals and objectives, it helps align the efforts of all stakeholders toward a common vision.

2. **Resource allocation:** The plan assists in allocating resources effectively. It helps identify critical areas where investments in finances, manpower, technology, or other resources are needed.

3. **Risk management:** The plan assesses potential risks and challenges, enabling the company to develop effective strategies to mitigate these risks. It also allows for proactive decision-making to navigate uncertainties and market fluctuations.

4. **Performance measurement:** The plan establishes metrics and key performance indicators (KPIs) to evaluate the company's progress towards its goals. This facilitates regular monitoring and allows for adjustments if the company deviates from its intended path.

5. **Communication and alignment:** The plan serves as a communication tool. Internally, it ensures that all employees understand the company's objectives and their roles in achieving them. Externally, it communicates the company's vision and direction to stakeholders, including investors, customers, and partners.

6. **Adaptability and flexibility:** The plan sets a strategic direction for the company but allows flexibility to adapt to changing market conditions and emerging opportunities. It's not set in stone; rather, it serves as a dynamic framework that can be adjusted as needed.

7. **Competitive Advantage** helps the company identify its unique strengths and opportunities for differentiation in the market. By leveraging these advantages effectively, the company can gain a competitive edge over rivals.

I can't believe that having studied all this, I hadn't thought about the significance of strategic planning since I got my MBA!

My eyes light on another page of notes from my course.

Critical Elements of an Effective Strategic Plan

Typically, several elements provide a comprehensive framework for guiding the organization toward its goals. Essential elements of a strategic plan can include:

1. The **Vision Statement**, which concisely describes the long-term aspirations and goals of the organization— provides a clear picture of what the organization aims to achieve in the future.

2. The **Mission Statement**, which outlines the fundamental purpose and core values of the organization—defines the organization's reason for existence and its primary objectives.

3. The **Values and Culture** section, which articulates the core values and beliefs that guide the behavior and decision-making within the organization. It defines the organizational culture and sets expectations for how employees interact and conduct themselves.

4. The **SWOT Analysis**, which assesses the organization's *strengths, weaknesses, opportunities, and threats (SWOT)*. It helps identify internal strengths and weaknesses as well as external opportunities and threats that might impact the organization's ability to achieve its objectives.

5. **Goals and Objectives:** *Goals* are broad, overarching statements that describe what the organization aims to achieve, while *objectives* are specific, measurable targets that support the goals. Remember! Goals and objectives should be SMART (Specific, Measurable, Achievable, Relevant, and Time-bound).

6. **Strategies and Initiatives:** *Strategies* outline the organization's approach to achieving its objectives. They're high-level plans that define the direction and scope of the organization's activities. *Initiatives* are specific actions or projects designed to implement the strategies.

7. **Key Performance Indicators (KPIs)** are measurable metrics used to track progress towards achieving the objectives. They provide a means of assessing performance and identifying areas for improvement.

8. The **Implementation Plan** details how the strategic plan will be executed. It includes the *timelines, responsibilities, resource allocation, and milestones* necessary to implement the plan effectively.

9. The **Risk Management Plan** identifies potential risks and challenges that may affect the successful execution of the strategic plan. It outlines strategies for mitigating risks and managing uncertainties.

10. The **Monitoring and Evaluation** framework defines how the strategic plan's progress will be _tracked and assessed_. It includes regular reviews and checkpoints to ensure that the organization stays on track and makes adjustments as needed.

11. The **Communication Plan** outlines how the company will communicate the strategic plan to both internal and external stakeholders. It ensures that everyone understands the vision, goals, and expectations associated with the plan.

12. The **Review and Update Process** section of the plan should include a process for regular review and update to ensure that the plan remains relevant and responsive to changing internal and external factors.

Good stuff! So helpful! I'm glad I've taken a little time to refresh the theory before reviewing our company's three-year plan. These notes remind me that a strategic plan isn't just a "nice-to-have" for a business. Although it can be adjusted according to evolving circumstances, **the strategic plan is fundamental to understanding why a company exists and making sure that all activities align with achieving specific goals**. It also specifies how successes (and failures) will be tracked and measured.

And all that makes it crystal clear that _my role as VP of HR is to make sure that those strategic aims turn into reality._

So now I'm ready to revisit the We Make Things Three-Year Strategic Plan. It's pretty detailed, containing most, if not all, of the sections described in my notes. But these are the sections I need to focus on right now:

We Make Things (WMT) Three-Year Strategic Plan

This overarching goal and set of objectives align with the organization's strategic objectives, providing a roadmap for achieving excellence and sustainable growth.

Overarching Goal

✓ Elevate Organizational Excellence and Growth

Objectives

1. Achieve a 25% increase in market share.
2. Attract and retain top talent.
3. Improve employee experience and boost eNPS (Employee Net Promoter Score).
4. Leverage technology for manufacturing excellence.
5. Enhance efficiency and achieve cost reduction.

Key Performance Indicators (KPIs):

Market Share Growth Rate

✓ Target: Achieve a 13% increase in market share within the next fiscal year.

Talent Acquisition and Retention

✓ KPI: Decrease time-to-fill for critical positions by 20%.
✓ KPI: Achieve an employee retention rate of 80% over the next year.

Employee Experience and eNPS

✓ KPI: Improve eNPS by 10 points year over year.

Technology Implementation and Efficiency

✓ KPI: Achieve a 10% increase in manufacturing efficiency year over year.
✓ KPI: Achieve a 10% increase in administrative efficiency year over year .

Cost Reduction:

✓ KPI: Achieve a cost reduction of 10% across manufacturing and administration operations year over year.
✓ KPI: Improve the cost-to-revenue ratio by 5% over the next fiscal year.

The first thing I notice is how vague the Overarching Goal or vision statement is. But two words stand out: Growth and Excellence.

Next, I review the Objectives and formulate future-facing questions. When I meet with the COO, these will help me get the details I'll need from her to define HR's role in achieving each objective.

Just to be clear, my primary objective in meeting with the COO is not to get answers to these and other questions. It's to get her support for creating a strategic HR plan that aligns the function with our overall business objectives. But asking myself questions like these will be a regular feature of my preparation for meetings in the future.

So, I continue reviewing the plan, thinking of questions that will lead me to the facts and data I'll need to inform the eventual HR plan.

After studying the company's Strategic Plan thoroughly and making lots of notes, I take care of the last remaining notes in my inbox then shut down my computer for the day, my mind full of new insights and information.

I head home to spend the evening with my partner and try to find some of that illusive work-life balance.

The next morning, I arrive at the office and gather my thoughts in preparation for meeting with my COO. At the appointed time, I walk into her office with confidence.

After preliminary greetings, I open by updating her on the HR conference.

"For me, the most powerful session, the one on how to **be** strategic, stressed the need for HR departments to be intimately connected to the achievement of a company's business plan—to help drive it towards success. It got me thinking about how we've been operating and whether I've really aligned the HR team to be totally focused on achieving WMTs objectives."

The COO raises her eyebrows. She hasn't been expecting this from me—I guess she thought I was just going to talk about how busy we all are and ask her to let me keep my team members.

I continue. "WMT needs to cut costs and improve the cost-to-revenue ratio by 5% over the next 12 months. You've asked me to lose a team member as part of the effort to reduce admin costs by 10%, which I'm committed to.

"However, as our overarching goal is to 'Elevate Organizational Excellence and Growth,' I also need to ensure that my team is in good shape to play our part in moving the company forward. We need to focus on supporting the company's growth, and that starts with developing 'organizational excellence' in my department.

"That's why I'm asking for your support. I want to create a comprehensive three-year strategic plan for HR that aligns with the company's goals. I want to reshape my team and define our goals for the year ahead."

She has been listening with surprise—and interest. Rather than challenging me, she agrees. "Danielle, that actually sounds great. So, how much time do you think you'll need to come up with your proposal?"

Relieved, I take a deep breath and switch gears to talk about logistics and process. "I'll need time to reach out to the exec team so I can align our department's activities with what they need from HR to achieve each of their objectives. My team will be helping me to gather data, of course, and doing a lot of the research. But while we're putting everything together, we still have to make sure the department provides a good service to everyone and to keep up our daily responsibilities."

She nods but is still waiting for my answer. "Okay, I understand— so, how much time do you think you'll need to come up with this proposal? Right now, we're setting the budgets for next year, so I'll need your proposal within ten days at the latest."

That's a tight deadline, but I must show I can do this.

"Okay, I'll have drafted the strategy for your review by then. If you approve, we in HR can prepare a presentation to communicate everything to the exec team within a day or so."

She agrees and tells me to come to her for help if I get stuck. I don't intend for that to happen, but before we close the meeting, I dive into the details of the company strategy and get her to clarify the objectives. I want to be 100% certain that I've got the priorities right so I can understand the resources that I'll need to help achieve them.

"For example, for the objective 'Achieve a 25% increase in market share,' how do you see this happening? Will the company achieve this by strengthening the Sales & Marketing team? Or via a marketing campaign led by an external agency? Or by designing and launching new products?"

Without waiting for a response, I go on. "Likewise, for the objective 'Attract and retain top talent': Did the exec team have a specific group in mind when they set this objective? How did they define 'top talent'?"

As I go through the list of future-facing questions I'd prepared, the conversation takes a new direction. She seems happy to clarify the objectives and refer me to the key people I should reach out to so I could gain a better understanding of what's already in place and where solutions were still needing to be defined.

As I head back to my office, I'm feeling supercharged: pleased with how the meeting has gone and determined to make the changes happen.

Here's how I see my role: I'll spend time with key stakeholders—my peers—to ensure that we're capturing everything the company needs from HR. In the meantime, my team members will do their own research and work on ideas to achieve those KPIs in ways that enable us to make the greatest impact in the medium-to-long term.

There's a lot to get done.

So, on to Point #3 on my to-do list: Now, I have to get the team on board. *This is where I need to step up and become their leader by speaking strategically.*

I schedule a team meeting for later this afternoon. I don't give them many details about the topic other than to tell them we're going to create a strategic plan for HR.

Before we meet, I want to make sure I'm prepared. Since my facilitation skills are pretty rusty, I use some of my 'strategic thinking' time to brush up on techniques for effectively guiding the discussion as their team leader. I give thanks and praise to LinkedIn and YouTube for putting some incredible resources at my fingertips.

I'm planning to use the Socratic inquiry techniques I've been practicing with Sam and Luisa to make sure that everyone's input gets heard and understood—and to avoid falling into the trap of saying, 'I have the solution.'

Because I want to get this right, I draft a meeting plan.

Thinking Strategically: Meeting Preparation.

1. **Clarify meeting objectives**

   ✓ Clearly define the objectives of the meeting. What do I want to achieve by the end of the session?

   ✓ How will I ensure that team members understand the significance of WMT's 3-year plan and their role in contributing to the departmental strategic plan?

2. **Create a structured agenda**

   ✓ Outline a clear agenda for the meeting, breaking down key topics and activities into manageable segments.

   ✓ Allocate time for team discussions, brainstorming sessions, and decision-making processes.

3. **Leverage team dynamics**

   ✓ Consider my team's dynamics, including their personalities, communication styles, and areas of expertise.
   ✓ Anticipate potential challenges or barriers to effective collaboration, and plan strategies to address them.

4. **Prepare meeting materials**

   ✓ Develop the slides I'll need to guide the discussion and keep the team focused on key topics.

Speaking Strategically: Facilitating the Meeting

1. **Establish meeting ground rules**

   ✓ Set ground rules for the meeting to ensure that discussions remain focused, respectful, and productive.
   ✓ Encourage active participation and open communication.

2. **Encourage ownership and accountability**

   ✓ **Emphasize the importance of each team member's contribution to the strategic planning process.**

   ✓ Encourage ownership of ideas and decisions, and establish accountability for implementing the strategic HR plan.

3. **Address potential resistance**

   ✓ Anticipate potential resistance or skepticism from team members, and be prepared to address their concerns with empathy and transparency.
   ✓ Highlight the benefits of strategic planning and how it will contribute to the department's success.

Acting Strategically: Follow-Up and Next Steps

1. **Schedule regular check-ins or progress reviews to ensure that the HR strategic plan is completed by the deadline!**

2. **Emphasize that for the next eight working days, everyone's top priority is to be delivering an HR plan that's aligned with the company business plan.**

Although I'm satisfied with my facilitation plan, something keeps nagging at the back of my mind, making me uncomfortable. The COO's previous instruction to cut one of my team members hasn't been addressed.

I remember Simone Grant, the speaker at the conference, stressing the need for integrity and authenticity to build trust. Yet, here I am, wrestling with that age-old HR dilemma—do I share the possibility that one of them might be leaving my team—and destabilize them? Or do I say nothing right now in the hope that our new strategic direction might mean that I won't need to lose a team member?

For now, I decide to say nothing. I'm convinced that, since the company's aim is 'organizational excellence and growth,' I can make a strong case for aligning each team member with a specific strategic objective. By streamlining our processes to increase efficiency—for example, reducing our recruitment expenses and lengthy times-to-hire, both of which impact the smooth operation of the business—I can still achieve the cost optimization required by the company's strategic plan.

At 2 pm, we all head to a meeting room, Laura leading the way, chatting in her normal amiable manner that makes her so good in her recruiting role. She's obviously trying to lighten the mood since no was sure what I meant by an HR Strategic Plan.

Josh, the thoughtful Compensation Analyst, gently interrupts as we walk and asks what everyone is wondering: "Why the sudden focus on a strategic plan, Danielle?"

"Great question!" exclaims Mike. "To be honest, as an Employee Relations Specialist, I'm not even sure I know what that means!" His boisterous laugh fills the hallway.

"You're not alone," smiles Anna, the HR and Payroll Specialist

I turn and give the team a sweeping grin as we walk into the meeting room. As we settle, I open by setting the context. "Thanks for taking the time to join me today. I know you have work waiting for you back on your desks, but this is a critical moment for us.

"Everyone knows that HR is an efficient department. We're busy, and we support everyone who needs our help. But I think you'd agree that, somehow, we're not really viewed as part of the real business."

Heads tilt and nod. Mike speaks up in agreement. "Yeah, you're right! People talk about us as if we're doing nothing, but we're busy all the time."

"Well, today it's time to change that perception," I announce. "We are an essential part of the company, and we have a vital role to play in helping We Make Things grow and be successful.

"So, as we move into this new fiscal year, I think it's time for us to align our efforts with the company's strategic plan. What do you already know about WTM's 3-Year Business Plan?"

Silence. Shrugging shoulders, shaking heads. "You know, Danielle, we talk about this, and we as a team were discussing it earlier—and we have never even thought about the plan," states Josh.

I share the slides and give them a few moments to read through them.

"Let me be open with you. Until recently, I'd hardly thought about it, either. After all, HR is busy. We're efficient. We get on and deliver whatever we're asked to provide.

"But I've realized that this plan is *the entire reason HR exists as a function*. Our sole purpose is to help the business achieve its overarching aim—to **elevate operational excellence and growth**. This goal is supported by several key objectives, which we can go over briefly today."

I click to the next slide that states the objectives.

"Our first objective is to achieve a 25% increase in market share. That's an ambitious target and will require concerted efforts from all departments. So, my question to you is—what should the HR team do to make this happen?"

Lauren, the Talent Acquisition Manager, is the first to speak. "Well, it's my job to make sure we're attracting and retaining the right talent to drive this growth."

I nod and smile. "Exactly, Lauren. Is there anything you could be doing to make our recruitment more effective, specifically to support this goal?"

She looks around and back to me, thoughtful. "Well, I guess right now, I mainly recruit on the basis of ad-hoc requests from the managers. I haven't really been working with them to define the resources they're likely to need to meet that 25%. And people don't realize that to attract and bring in even one high-potential employee takes a mountain of work, and it can take weeks or even months."

Josh chimes in. "And although we have the annual headcount plan and budget, in practice, we don't really monitor how well we're sticking to it. Turnover has costs, and when we lose people, we may have to pay more to replace them—and not only that, but it has a negative impact on production and quality since we're trying to grow market share."

The discussion continues around that 25% market share objective, and I'm pleased to see that the team is so willing to play a part in "owning" it—acquiring, developing, and retaining the people we will need to reach that target.

After a while, I move the discussion on. "So, we agree that attracting and retaining top talent is our overriding objective. With Lauren leading our talent acquisition efforts, we have a strong foundation, but what are the kinds of things we can do to build a strong leadership pipeline to meet the demands of our growth targets over the coming years?"

Next, Mike, the Employee Relations and Compliance Specialist, contributes. "I think we have to look at retaining our talent first. You know, I do an exit interview with every employee who leaves. What happens to that information? What lessons do we learn? Sure, some people complain about their compensation, but the number one thing I hear is that *there's no career development here*. No one is nurturing the generation coming up, so they're moving on, and we lose everything we've invested in them. How can we grow with this constant churn?"

Anna, the HR Generalist, agrees. "That's totally true. If we want to keep the best people, we have to start taking action to provide what they tell us they need. We have to work on ways to improve the employee experience if we're going to boost that eNPS, the Employee Net Promoter Score. We need to create an environment where employees feel valued and engaged."

She continues as she feels the nods and support around her. "I hear a lot of complaints about the way some of the supervisors are treating the younger employees. It's not 1994, and we need to handle people with respect! And we keep losing our young leaders to the competition because of the career development other companies promise them."

Mike interjects, "That's all true, Anna, but *how can HR create the company culture*? Surely, that comes from the top and involves every single department!"

I step into the discussion. "You're right, Mike. And that's where the Strategic Plan comes in. What I need is for each—and all—of us to start focusing on these strategic objectives and thinking of how we can drive the change that Objective #3 requires. How we can align our efforts with those of the other departments to create this new culture? Each one of you will be taking ownership of the new way of working—and the results."

The discussion continues around the Objective #4: **leveraging technology for manufacturing excellence.** We agree that this will require collaboration between HR and other departments to ensure that the company's workforce is equipped with the necessary skills and tools to maximize efficiency.

Finally, since we're aiming to enhance efficiency and achieve cost reduction across the board, I want them to be ultra-clear that this will involve *streamlining HR processes, identifying areas for improvement, and implementing cost-saving measures wherever possible*.

Again, I open the floor for discussion and encourage them to think creatively. "How do you see our team contributing to these objectives, and what challenges do you anticipate?"

By the end of the meeting, I've achieved my objective—to change the focus of HR from being supportive-yet-isolated from the heart of the business to becoming strategic and transformational.

The team heads off, buzzing with ideas focused on creating the HR plan. I've offered them any support they need. They understand that I have to deliver the draft of the HR Strategic Plan in just ten days, so they need to do their research and give me their proposals by this time next week.

Over the next few days, the team seems to be on fire. I'm thrilled to see that they're not only brainstorming and collaborating with each other but also reaching out to every part of the company to collect information about how HR could make the greatest contribution to WMT's objectives.

Occasionally, one or more team member comes to me to get my steer on an issue or a possible solution, and I help by harnessing the power of those future-facing questions I've been practicing. I let them explore the alternatives and recommend the best answer.

I never allow them to forget the need to reduce costs in line with the company's overall 10% goal. Because we're already in the budgeting phase, anything they propose has to be properly costed—and the benefits evaluated.

Of course, I'm busy, too. I meet with executive team members to understand where they were going regarding their people-related strategic challenges—whether in terms of resources, capability, retention, or culture. I also make time for external research, such as local and national HR trends and best practices. I want to take my inspiration from the best thought leaders in the industry.

The daily meeting changes from a routine update about daily tasks to an opportunity for the team members to share what they are learning and suggest how we might address the challenges in the future.

One week later, with my team's help, I have a draft HR Strategic Plan to guide the department for the next three years. *I'm so proud of them—and myself. This was a lot to accomplish in just ten days.*

THREE-YEAR HR STRATEGIC PLAN TO SUPPORT ORGANIZATIONAL EXCELLENCE AND GROWTH

Objective 1: Talent Acquisition And Retention

A. Develop a comprehensive talent acquisition plan

1. Align recruitment strategies with organizational growth objectives.
2. Leverage cutting-edge recruitment technologies for efficient talent sourcing and screening.
3. Implement data-driven decision-making processes in talent acquisition.

B. Enhance WMT's employer brand

1. Position the organization as an employer of choice through targeted employer branding initiatives.
2. Utilize digital channels for employer branding and communication.
3. Implement initiatives to showcase a positive workplace culture and employee success stories.

C. Innovate onboarding and employee management systems

1. Integrate advanced onboarding systems for a seamless and engaging employee experience.
2. Implement employee management systems to streamline HR processes and enhance efficiency.
3. Leverage technology for continuous improvement in the employee lifecycle. Create a dashboard with goals and opportunities.

Objective 2: Employee Experience and Engagement

A. Track and improve the Employee Net Promoter Score (eNPS)

1. Conduct regular employee surveys and feedback sessions for insights into employee sentiments.
2. Utilize data analytics to identify trends and areas for improvement in employee experience.
3. Implement targeted initiatives to enhance workplace satisfaction, well-being, and engagement.

B. Utilize digital tools for communication and collaboration

1. Use digital communication tools to enhance real-time communication.
2. Implement collaboration platforms for seamless teamwork and knowledge sharing.
3. Provide digital tools for professional development opportunities and continuous learning.
4. Monitor and measure the impact of digital tools on overall employee satisfaction.

Objective 3: Strategic HR Technologies

A. Leverage HR analytics platforms:

1. Integrate advanced HR analytics platforms for data-driven decision-making.
2. Leverage analytics to align HR strategies with organizational goals.

B. Propose and implement technologies supporting HR initiatives.

1. Implement innovative recruitment technologies.

2. Optimize and harness the full potential of implemented HR platforms to achieve organizational goals.
3. Ensure seamless integration with other HR technologies for efficiency.

Objective 4: Employee Development and Performance Alignment

A. Implement an employee development and review process

1. Create a three-month initial training plan for every new recruit, with progress reviews monthly.
2. Ensure that each employee has an Individual Development Plan, with progress reviews quarterly.

B. Align employee work with the WMT strategic plan

1. Establish a robust process to align individual employee goals with the organization's strategic plan.
2. Integrate key performance indicators (KPIs) to measure individual contributions toward strategic objectives.

C. Provide development opportunities for employees

1. Provide training for supervisors in coaching and team leadership.
2. Create "fast-track" development plans for high-potential employees.
3. Identify skill gaps through regular assessments and provide targeted training and development opportunities.
4. Foster a culture of continuous learning to prepare employees for the future of work.

D. Develop programs to upskill employees for the future

1. Develop a framework for upskilling employees in emerging technologies and future-oriented skills.
2. Implement mentorship and coaching programs to support employee growth and readiness for evolving roles.

E. Integrate the employee development and review processes

1. Collaborate with HR Technology and Analytics Coordinator to implement digital tools for performance tracking and individual development plans.
2. Integrate employee development goals into the onboarding and employee management systems for a holistic approach to talent management.

Well! The time has come to share the results of our collective work with the team.

"I love this!" exclaims Laura. "It's so great to see how the work I do is part of something bigger."

"I agree," says Josh thoughtfully. "Setting these goals will help us prioritize our projects when so much comes at us every day."

At first, they're blown away. It's all new and exciting—a world away from the daily routines they can perform with their eyes shut.

But it's still somewhat abstract and "big picture." I need to be more specific about what these changes will mean for them, in reality.

Anna confirms my thoughts. "I have to admit I don't really see how these goals will affect our daily work."

So, I decide to also share the KPIs I've developed to ensure that our team's progress will have specific targets and that our success can be measured.

KPIs RELATED TO HR STRATEGIC PLAN

Talent Acquisition and Retention

- ✓ Achieve an employee retention rate of 80% over the next year.
- ✓ Achieve a 30% reduction in time-to-fill critical positions through advanced recruitment technologies.

Employee Experience and eNPS

- ✓ Improve eNPS by 10 points year over year.
- ✓ Enhance overall employee satisfaction through the utilization of digital communication and collaboration tools.

Alignment with Strategic Goals

- ✓ Achieve a 90% alignment between individual employee goals and the organization's strategic plan this fiscal year. *Measurement*: Regular audits and assessments of individual goals against strategic objectives.

Employee Engagement in Development Programs

- ✓ Ensure a participation rate of 80% in ongoing training and development opportunities. *Measurement*: Tracking attendance and engagement metrics for training sessions and development programs.

Effectiveness of Mentorship Programs

- ✓ Achieve a satisfaction rate of 90% among employees participating in mentorship programs. *Measurement*: Regular surveys and feedback on the quality and impact of mentorship relationships.

Feedback Integration

✓ Implement feedback from 80% of employees into individual development plans. *Measurement*: Systematic integration of employee feedback into personalized development strategies.

Efficiency in Performance Reviews

✓ Reduce the time spent on performance reviews by 20% while maintaining effectiveness. *Measurement*: Evaluation of the time taken for performance review processes.

Technology Implementation and Efficiency

✓ Achieve a 10% increase year over year in HR process efficiency through technology adoption.

Cost Reduction

✓ Achieve a cost reduction of 10% in HR processes year over year.
✓ Improve the HR cost-to-revenue ratio by 5% over the next fiscal year.

This is all getting a bit more real for them, and the questions start coming.

Lauren is the first to question her KPIs. "Does this mean you want me to achieve a 30% reduction in time-to-fill critical positions through advanced recruitment technologies?" With excitement in her voice, she continues, "What advanced recruitment technologies can I have to support me?"

"Good questions," I respond. "Right now, we're all using pretty basic tools for our processes, and as you can see, virtually every KPI will require us to leverage technology to achieve the efficiency and cost-savings we're targeting. So, I want you to work as a team, research the HR platforms on the market, and develop a recommendation for products that will be able to transform the way we work.

"Reach out to IT for their support and advice, as they'll be involved in any implementation project. But remember, whatever you recommend has to serve HR, so don't compromise on functionality. And cost out every option so I can make a recommendation to the COO."

Anna chimes in. "There are some great HR platforms out there now, and I've been dreaming about having one that would help me cut down on routine admin."

Mike adds, "Agreed, we waste so much time tracking the online training and following up to make sure people get it done."

This has really gotten them engaged. I try to channel their energy. "Right, so look for the best-in-class products for companies with our profile. Whatever platforms we go for have to transform the way we work—as well as being cost-effective."

"I'm a bit concerned," admits Lauren. "In my last company, they designed a system in-house. It took almost a year, was full of glitches, and cost a fortune in consultancy and maintenance."

Josh has a solution. "Listen, we need something that's really simple to implement and use. Something that allows the employees to access their data directly to cut down the amount of time we spend responding to routine queries. Why use time and resources designing something when there are great products out there that can be implemented with minimal effort?"

We all agree, so I move them on. "Great. Now your task is to come up with a proposal that will transform the way we work, freeing up time for all of you and helping to change the way we interact with our employees. This will impact the KPI related to enhancing overall employee satisfaction through the utilization of digital communication and collaboration tools."

The energetic discussion continues. The team highlights the time and effort required to set up and roll out a company-wide mentorship program. Some are concerned about the KPI related to performance reviews and individual development plans. Lauren points out the lack of focus on high-potential talent. *At this stage, I don't have any way to reassure her.*

When it's time to wrap up the meeting, I summarize. "While we may need to review the KPIs, do you agree we should aim for the draft Strategic Plan for HR? Are you willing to work to achieve it?"

They agree that they are.

A wave of relief passes through me. "Awesome. Now, I want you all to be clear that the way you work, and more importantly, the way you think about your role, is going to change dramatically. We're all going to have to change our focus and step up to reach these goals.

"And there's one other thing we're all going to have to accept—it won't be possible to please everyone. We can't continue to be the company's drop-in-and-vent center. Sometimes, this will feel uncomfortable. How will you handle that transition?"

Mike speaks up. "Well, my role will still involve dealing face-to-face with people and helping them resolve their issues, but I can definitely be more organized in how I allocate my time—and also how I follow up on feedback so that the same issues won't come up again and again."

Josh is also ready for a change. "It would be great if I didn't spend so much time constantly answering questions about compensation. If people could just access their own data, I could focus more on analytics, and we could use data to drive our decisions."

Anna adds, "I'd love it if employees could be able to check their vacations online, without constantly having to ask me."

And Lauren adds to the wish list as well. "I'd love it if the managers could track the progress of their recruitment needs without constantly calling me for updates. And if I could cut down on the time I spend on applications that don't even meet our basic requirements."

I'm only just now realizing how many of their concerns could be addressed by implementing new technology.

"Remember, for every new platform we implement," I point out, "we have to be able to justify its impact on the bottom line. We have to demonstrate what we will be doing with the time that has been freed up, and how our actions will align with the HR plan—and so with WTM's 3-Year Plan."

As we close the meeting, I'm feeling energized by their enthusiasm and how far we've already come on the journey to transform HR into a future-facing department.

My next step is to achieve Point #5 on my initial To-Do list: Speak strategically to the COO.

So that's exactly what I do when I'm able to schedule a meeting with her the following day. She seems receptive as I run through the draft HR plan, linking each objective to those in WMT's 3-Year Plan. I emphasize the need for the HR department to harness technology to streamline our processes, free up our resources, and serve the company more efficiently.

While she agrees in principle with what I'm proposing, she has three caveats. The first is that I need to show her a revised structure for the HR team that will be capable of delivering our objectives.

Second, I need to bring her a detailed, costed-out proposal for the new HR/IT solutions. She recommends that I work closely with IT and Finance on this. She's surprised when I tell her that my team is already on it—they've put together a task force, not only from those departments but including stakeholders from around the company. That will help make sure we'll be delivering a service that responds to those departments' day-to-day needs and frees them from routine employee-related admin as well.

Caveat #3 is that I still need to achieve that 10% cost reduction. New IT will be expensive, and although we can discuss where that expense is allocated, I still need to reduce my budget to justify it and prove a return on investment.

I'd anticipated all these points, and I agree to them.

I've achieved my objective for the meeting and feel I'm almost "there." Now, onto the next step, which is restructuring the department.

Reflections for the Reader

1. THINK

- ✓ What are the most pressing business challenges or opportunities facing my HR team today?
- ✓ What are the roadblocks I face in achieving the KPIs on my HR plan? How am I going to remove these, and what support will I need?
- ✓ How do I leverage my education and qualifications in my current role? Am I committed to life-long learning? What are the key skills I still need to develop, and how will I go about this?

2. SPEAK

- ✓ Does the way I communicate reflect my role as team leader? In team meetings, what proportion of time is spent discussing the future versus routine topics?
- ✓ How am I encouraging strategic thinking and problem-solving among my team?

3. ACT

- ✓ Danielle created her plan in just over a week. How much time would be realistic for me to do a similar exercise? Do I set realistic deadlines for major projects, with adequate time for information gathering, drafting, critiquing, and revising? Or do I prioritize a fast response time over quality?

CHAPTER

8

NAVIGATING THE UNKNOWN

Vision without action is merely a dream.
Action without vision just passes the time.
Vision with action can change the world.

— *Joel A. Barker*

Sam sets his strategy in motion

Back at Head Office, my first challenge is to connect with the CEO. His assistant tells me his schedule is packed, but he's sometimes willing to have people join him for a 6 a.m. breakfast. Although I'm exhausted after months of sleepless nights with our new baby, this first meeting is a make-or-break for me, and I agree without hesitation.

Two days later, over a plate of eggs, bacon, and avocado, washed down with an unidentifiable drink that tastes vaguely of pineapple, he asks me how it's going.

I describe how impressed I am—not only by the incredible technical expertise of the senior team but also by their energy. They've told me endless stories about the good old days when they were ready to take on the world.

He doesn't show emotion as he listens, which surprises me since he's known as an expressive guy.

This could be my best opportunity to listen and learn, so I fall silent and wait.

"Right, these guys are the best in the business. Apart from Jason (the CFO), we've been together for years, since college. Those early days were fantastic—honestly, I miss them.

"But now, I've got to think about WAT's future. Thirteen hundred employees depend on me, and the investors expect me to make money for them. We're heading for an IPO. I can't afford for this company to fail."

I nod in concern as I ask, "But your team is totally behind you? They've all told me how you're the best and they'll do anything for you."

He looks off in thought, then returns to me. "In their way, they do back me. But they still want to do what we were doing in those early days. They get an idea, convince themselves it's brilliant, and fight each other to accept it. They fight with me to get it accepted. Sometimes, they'll go ahead with an idea and tell me about it later when it's too late to say I don't accept it. I feel like we're back in school."

He shifts in his seat as his face becomes more worried. "Then there's Jason, who's been warning me for the past year that we can't count on our stellar results continuing. And I know the big players are waiting in the wings, just waiting for their moment.

"I'm sending the message out on TV, in podcasts, and in the financial press that WAT isn't about transforming companies—we're going to disrupt entire industries!

"But unless we develop new products and secure the investment needed to grow and strengthen, the competition will swoop in like wolves and devour us."

Listening attentively, I respond with compassion. "That's a lot to deal with. I've seen the strategic plan you put in place a couple of years back. How's that going?"

He looks confused.

"Oh yeah, that. So, um," he abruptly changes the subject. "How was your breakfast? Sorry, but I've got to get to my next meeting, but let's talk again soon." He rises from the table.

And he's gone.

I reflect on what I've learned. *That was strange and evasive*. However, I'm pleased, and a little surprised, that he opened up to me so quickly.

It's clear that, regardless of the act he puts on in front of the cameras, he's conscious that the company is facing potentially existential problems. He's frustrated by the in-fighting. While his team acknowledges him as the leader, he's confirmed that there's rivalry and that some of them even challenge him. He's still determining how to lead them and hasn't clarified where they're going.

Regarding my four imperatives for military success, *it's not looking good*. The command structure isn't clear. The objectives aren't communicated clearly, if at all. The 'hardware'—the products—are in place, but only for now. And his team members don't have each other's backs.

So, in our future conversations, I will have to "speak truth to power" and paint a picture of possible future scenarios, depending on his choices.

To my surprise, his calendar suddenly opens up for further meetings with me.

At the next breakfast meeting, as I share some of my battlefield stories to start a discussion about strategy and tactics, he begins to open up and vent his frustrations. We're starting to build a relationship of trust, but I can't afford to "lose" him by pushing too hard too soon.

Instead, I decide to tell him about my "strategic challenge." I raise the topic.

"You know, I've got to come up with next year's budget for HR. I've been speaking to the department heads about what they need, and they're all giving me their wish lists—more people, larger travel budgets for conferences, salary increases, bigger bonuses. To be honest, they think I'm here to make them all happy." I chuckle, a bit nervously.

"Tell me about it," he laughs. "One reason why I agreed to bring you in as CHRO was to stop people bugging me all the time about what they deserve. Now, it's your job to handle all that!"

We laugh. *I don't disagree, but I want to speak strategically.*

"Indeed! What's hard, though, is how to make sure that whatever we invest in our people from now on adds value to the company."

He agrees. "Of course, you're HR—not Santa Claus!"

I laugh but then continue in a serious tone. "But my dilemma is that I don't have anything concrete to base my decisions on. As a senior executive, I'm accountable for what HR spends. If I'm ever questioned about it, I have to account for every dollar."

"Right," he agrees. "Going for an IPO, we're all going to be questioned about our priorities, about how wisely we spend our investors' money."

"I've spent the past month getting to understand where the company is right now—our starting point, if you like," I explain.

"Okay...," he says questioningly.

"But, what's not clear to me is where we're trying to get to? You know, I'm a military guy. I need to understand: What's our mission?"

"Okay...," he repeats, encouraging me to keep talking.

I continue, knowing I have his attention. "Once I'm clear about these two things—*where we are today* and *where we want to be*—I can decide what steps the HR department needs to take to get there! I can take care of the tactics to achieve our objective—making sure any money we invest in our people brings a return on that investment and moves us closer to our goal. That way, HR can add real value to the company. That way, I can make sure that every step we take aligns with the mission that you, as the leader, set for WAT."

"Makes sense," he says, slightly nodding as he thinks. He's listening and letting me vent without interrupting my flow.

"But over the past few weeks," I assert, "I've realized that getting a handle on where we want to go wouldn't help just me—it would help the whole exec team get aligned and create a solid foundation for the company's future.

"Imagine if we all had the same goal. We could start having each other's backs instead of wasting time and energy infighting.

"Using data to measure progress would allow us to see what is moving us faster to our goals and what isn't creating the impact we need. It would allow us to focus our resources on what's important," I say emphatically.

He seems thoughtful. "I see where you're going with this, Sam. You want me to create a plan. But, you know…," he wavers. I prepare for his objection.

After a pause, he continues. "Well, um, WAT's strength is that we've always been agile. Sometimes, our best ideas have come out of nowhere. And there have been a few times when the environment's changed without warning, like during Covid, and because of our fluid structure, we've been able to pivot, outsmarting the competition and setting the media on fire!"

He's still musing. "We're still a young company, and I don't want to kill the creative, entrepreneurial spirit by imposing a plan that everyone has to, is required to, follow. It wouldn't fit our culture. It wouldn't be our brand. They'd hate it, and so would I."

I expected some pushback, so here it is. Hmm. Actually, I'm glad he's expressing his doubts. I need to affirm him first, without getting defensive. "I get that. I do! I understand the need for agility, especially with such a talented team. But doesn't that carry a risk? I mean, if things keep shifting daily, we might end up with everyone moving in different directions.

"The outcome? A lot of action, plenty of fireworks, but zero tangible progress. All our efforts could end up scattered and fading to nothing. *And that's exactly what we need to avoid.* I think that a plan could help get us all moving in the same direction so we reach where you want us to be, making the best use of our time and resources. Don't you?"

He ponders what I'm saying. After I give him some thinking time, I decide to use one of the examples from my research. "It makes me think about Juicero. We can't make the same mistakes as they did."

"Juicero?" he queries.

"True story. It was a startup founded in 2013 that claimed to be disrupting the juicing industry with its beautifully designed high-tech juicer and subscription-based model."

"Before my time, but like WAT, in some ways?" he asks.

"In certain respects, yes. They raised massive funding and generated hype around their product. It was marketed as a sleek, high-end appliance capable of producing fresh juice from proprietary juice packs. The marketing campaign was way ahead of its time, and Juicero machines were on the way to becoming a celebrity must-have."

"Sounds good. Who doesn't love juice? But what happened?"

I am in storytelling mode. "One day, someone realized that this $400 machine was essentially unnecessary. That you could achieve the same result by squeezing the juice packs with your hands."

He laughs out loud as I continue. "So, of course, Juicero was ridiculed, and the company failed practically overnight. The question is—how could that happen? Why did nobody see that coming? Solid finance, talented team, brilliant design, awesome marketing.

"But they were all so focused on their own areas of expertise and their own priorities, there was no strategic thinking. Their priorities were so misaligned that they missed the basic reality: They weren't delivering meaningful value to customers."

"And they only had that one product?" my CEO asks, incredulous.

"Right! Yes. And we also have to ask—where was their plan for the future? Because of course, even if the product had been good, a copycat company would have soon cloned it and produced at lower cost to grab market share from Juicero."

From there, we swap more stories about startups that have crashed and burned in the past few years. Quibi, MoviePass, FNX, even Theranos. Initially lauded as entrepreneurial geniuses, their founders are now languishing in obscurity or in prison.

These spectacular falls from grace play on his mind more than he cares to admit.

"I get where you're going with this," he acknowledges. "I know where I want the company to be in the next five years, ten years even, so maybe it's time to make sure the whole team knows."

He's getting it. I seize my advantage. "Would it help the company if we were to create a fresh new plan that sets the direction? A strategy that's about starting right where we are now, envisioning the future we want, and planning how to get there. One that clarifies where we want to get to and keeps everyone going in the same direction."

"I get it. You're absolutely right. Yes, Sam, let's create that plan! As long as we don't kill the spirit of WAT in the process."

I reassure him. "We'll ensure that it's broad-brush, allowing us to stay agile and flexible enough to respond to our challenges. We'll also check in periodically, crunch the numbers, and analyze the data so we can adjust the priorities according to what's happening in the world and then recalibrate our actions along the way to reaching the goal."

"That sounds about right. You know, I'll have to convince the team that I'm serious about this since it'll create a new way of working. Otherwise, they'll revert to their same old ways."

"What if I present the project of co-creating a strategic plan to the team—and convince them of the advantages?"

"I'd be good with that," he says agreeably.

"And think about it. One of the biggest advantages for you of defining your mission and creating a measurable plan is that when priorities are clear, you can step back. You won't be constantly called on to make urgent decisions or resolve disputes. By making the team accountable and giving them ownership of the results, you'll harness their problem-solving potential."

"That would sure take a weight off my shoulders and free up my time."

"Your exec team can get on with running the company, which is what they're very well paid to do, and you'll finally be able to focus outwards towards the market—being the face and voice of the WAT brand as we gear up for the IPO."

"Okay, Sam, I'm sold. You've got my go ahead. What will you need from me?"

Yes! I did it! I try to contain my glee as I respond to him. "I'll need you to define your vision for WAT. Big picture. Why does it exist? What's the dream? That's going to be the starting point. I can help with that if you like."

"No, you're good," he replies. "Let me work on that, and I'll have it for you before you give your presentation. Any good examples to get me started?"

Naturally, thinking strategically, I'd prepared for this.

"I've always liked Google's vision: 'To organize the world's information and make it universally accessible and useful.' It's a nice blend of huge ambition and social engagement."

"Not bad. Any others?"

I check my notes: "Apple's is 'To bring the best user experience to its customers through its innovative hardware, software, and services.'

It's very specific about what it aims to achieve and how it's going to achieve it."

"It's good. Any more?"

He seems to be enjoying this, but I want to wrap up the conversation and let him think creatively. However, I've got one more to share.

"The Netflix vision statement is 'To entertain the world.'"

"Genius! Says it all in four words. Anything else you need from me, Sam?"

I think for a moment. "Well, I think this should be positioned as *your* meeting—the invite should come from you. It's got to be clear that you're driving this project since it's a major strategic initiative. I'll just be facilitating."

"I'll take care of that. You can count on it. Okay. Is that all?"

"For now, those two things are great. I'll take care of the rest."

He stares out of the window at the city skyline. He's smiling to himself. "I need to do something big to make it clear that I'm serious. And I think I know just how to grab their attention."

He turns to face me. "Dexter!"

But before I can ask, he's gone.

Reflections for the Reader

1. THINK

- ✓ As a CHRO, how do I view my role as a coach to the CEO?
- ✓ How do I strategically approach guiding and advising the CEO, particularly during times of organizational transition or growth?
- ✓ How do I communicate the strategic importance of HR to other executives? How do I position HR as a critical partner in shaping the organization's future?

2. SPEAK

- ✓ Think of a recent conversation where I had to influence others toward a strategic decision. How did I tailor my communication to ensure clarity and focus?
- ✓ How do I balance listening and speaking in strategic discussions to ensure that the conversation leads to actionable insights?

3. ACT

- ✓ Reflect on a time when I had to build rapport with a new leader or team member in a high-stakes situation. What strategies did I use, and how did this affect the outcome of my collaboration?
- ✓ When acting strategically, how do I make sure that my actions foster collaboration and open communication across departments or teams?
- ✓ How do I balance the need for decisive action with the importance of nurturing relationships, particularly when implementing a significant organizational change?

CHAPTER

9

THE THINK—SPEAK—ACT MODEL

*I can't change the direction of the wind,
but I can adjust my sails to always reach
my destination.*

— *Jimmy Dean*

Luisa continues her exploration

I reached out to Sasha McConnell, who's going to run the strategic planning meeting for my company.

I was pleasantly surprised when Sasha accepted my meeting request. She was coming to discuss the details of the planning meeting with our CEO in a couple of days and suggested that we block out some time to sit together so she could learn more about the role of HR at WFT and answer my questions about how I could approach the strategic planning meeting most effectively. I wanted her help to make sure that I made an impact.

I'd mentioned the Think-Speak-Act model, and she said she'd be interested to hear my thoughts on how it would relate to WFT's upcoming transformation.

When we finally sit down together, Sasha looks exactly as I would expect a high-flying MBA from an Ivy League school to look. She exudes confidence. Yet there is no arrogance about her—she seems warm and ready to listen. I'm hoping she'll be willing to share her insights.

In line with my new strategic thinking approach, I prepared well for the meeting. After briefly chatting about our respective backgrounds and the typical challenges HR leaders face, I start to explain.

"Since the recent conference I attended, I've been working on implementing the Think-Speak-Act model in almost every aspect of my HR role."

I begin by outlining my approach to becoming recognized and respected as a strategic player. I want my peers to understand how much I have to contribute as their business partner and how I can take an active role instead of passively waiting for instructions about how to support the other leaders.

"To think strategically, I'm now shifting my mindset and asking myself future-facing questions about myself, the company, and the transition, all to prepare myself for the meeting and the challenges beyond.

"This gives me a basis to speak strategically during the meeting— leading the discussions, asking the right questions, and being armed with the data I need to make proposals and contribute to the outcomes.

"I'm also considering how to act strategically after the meeting. I want to use all the 'needs' that we'll define in the meeting to develop an overall vision for HR's role in the next three years. Then, I can define action steps to achieve that vision and contribute to the successful evolution of the company."

Sasha has been listening patiently. "I'm impressed that you're preparing so assiduously for the meeting, Luisa! It seems you've got this—and you're ready to make a great contribution. So, what can I do to help you today?"

Good question. "I guess that although I've started thinking more strategically, I haven't really had the opportunity to test out my new approach. I've never been in this kind of meeting before, and it's my one chance to get it right. So, I'd welcome your input and advice. Am I on the right track? Will my approach work in practice? Where should I start?"

Sasha smiles. "That's always the hardest question! I'd say the fundamental question you need to ask yourself is: *What will need to change for the company to move from where it is today to achieve the vision?*"

"Everything will need to change! New departments—marketing, sales, logistics, training, the comp and bens structure, automation and AI systems…. That's why I get overwhelmed! Where will I start?"

Sasha's still smiling. "In my experience, it helps to *think in terms of impact, not tasks*. Prioritize whatever makes the greatest impact. And don't fall into the trap of going for 'sticking plasters' or 'low-hanging fruit.' That's a distraction. To think strategically, you need to look at delivering long-term value for the business, one year or three years down the line."

"That makes total sense," I reply. "Because once I've defined—with input from the CEO and my peers—what the company's priorities are, I can start to plan the steps to achieve each one. And that will form the basis of my strategic plan for HR."

"Right," nods Sasha. "Thinking strategically, before committing to any HR initiative, the question becomes: *Does it align with, and add value to, our direction? Does it contribute to the achievement of our vision?*"

I think about this for a second. It sounds great. However, from experience, I know that getting resources for HR initiatives can be challenging. For example, talent development is sometimes viewed as a luxury. So, I voice one of my "uncomfortable thoughts."

"I get what you're saying, Sasha. But how can I make sure that what I put in my plan remains a priority, when all the other directors also have their plans—and we're all vying for limited resources?"

"Hmm," she nods. "That's an age-old problem that all businesses face. And you know, HR people often complain that they're not considered connected to the business and that what they need is never considered a priority.

"But I like to turn it around," she continues. "What is HR doing to be part of the journey towards the vision? What is the business problem they're helping to solve? Have they evaluated it carefully? Have they explained the impact clearly?"

I feel a shock of recognition. I've certainly done my share of whining about being sidelined by my peers. "You know, until now, I never thought of it like that. But you're right. I need to be sure about the bottom-line value of anything I put in the HR plan. And more broadly, I need to prove that we in HR understand value."

She nods. "No other function in a business would expect to act without analyzing the impact of anything they do—in dollar terms and in terms of alignment with the strategic plan."

I reply thoughtfully. "There may be things I want to do that are aligned with our vision, but they won't make the required impact based on the investment, or we can't afford them any time soon. It's my responsibility to ensure that anything I propose is financially viable and impactful. I shouldn't wait until my budget request is rejected and then complain!"

"That's absolutely right, Luisa! So, *how are you going to ensure that your plan is based on actions that are impactful and support the bottom line of the business?*"

130

I try to think of a specific example. "Well, let's say I propose increasing the technician headcount. First, I should evaluate how much the current situation is costing or could cost the company if we don't act. I should be ready to back everything up with the potential financial benefits—let's say, for every technician hire, we'll bring in X dollars per year in additional revenue."

"And do you think taking that approach will help you to be seen as strategic?"

"Definitely. Sasha, you've given me plenty of ideas to help me think strategically as I prepare for the meeting. And since I've blocked off 90 minutes for preparation each day just to research and think strategically, I'll be arriving armed with some proposals—plus the data to back them up."

Sasha smiles at me reassuringly. "I love that you're taking this planning exercise so seriously and taking the time you need to get ready. The only word of caution I'd have is that, at this point, priorities aren't set in stone. Who knows what innovative ideas the team will come up with? So don't be too attached to your proposals—just focus on the facts that back them up."

Wise and sobering words. "Of course, I'm looking forward to co-creating the overall strategy with the others. It's an exciting moment to be part of. Thanks for helping me think that through, Sasha."

"It's my pleasure—I'm happy to help." She shifts gears a little. "Now, I think you mentioned you'd like to talk about how to make sure you make the right impact in the meeting itself."

Yes, that had been on my mind quite a bit. I wanted to present myself as a new, future-facing Luisa.

"Yes. Since that conference, I've realized it's time for a personal rebrand. I want to be seen as the natural choice to lead HR in the new organization. But will that mean ditching the old Luisa, who everybody loves and trusts—and who I also kind of love and enjoy being?"

Sasha takes a moment to consider her reply. "Over twenty years, you've built up your reputation. What is it that's made people love and trust you?"

"I think, deep down, I've always been myself. Because I've grown into my role over the years, I've never had to put on a show, a front. People know that with me, what you see is what you get. And they know I care about this company and the people here."

"So you're valued for your authenticity and integrity. There's no reason why you should lose those invaluable qualities. But as your role changes, as you become more focused on the future, *perhaps you'll need to let go of being everyone's best friend and perfect listener.*

"It may not be comfortable at first, but as you rebrand yourself to gain more respect from your peer group, you'll have to make some decisions about how you spend your time and what you delegate."

I laugh. "It's true. I have enjoyed being 'Momma Luisa' to just about everyone. But Rob, my HR Specialist, is also a great listener with a gift for making peace even in explosive situations. He can take over that mantle while I focus on aligning HR with the company vision. I'll share the changes with him so he'll understand the why, as well as the what, of the changes in our roles."

I'm still a little concerned about re-launching the 'Luisa brand' at the strategic planning meeting, so I take the opportunity to look for advice about how to make the best impact and earn the credibility I want from the CEO and the senior team.

"In terms of the meeting itself, I'm struggling with preparing my proposals. How can I know that my suggestions will be accepted?" I ask.

Sasha reassures me. "I would say that in this meeting, you shouldn't expect to make any concrete proposals. Without knowing the company's strategic aims, how can you know what's needed?"

She's right. I've been getting ahead of myself.

Sasha continues. "Instead, I would focus on asking questions— questions that facilitate creative thinking, that encourage people to look at issues from a different angle and that open up discussion. That way, you're already positioning yourself as a leader. And, when you have facts, data, and research, to contribute to the conversation, you will be making a powerful statement."

A lightbulb moment. I'll be judged on the quality of my questions that help us explore options and define the best solution, not necessarily on my ability to reveal pre-determined solutions that I've created in isolation.

"Have you ever heard of consultative selling?" asks Sasha.

I confess that I haven't.

She explains. "Consultative or needs-based selling is, as the name suggests, a sales technique where reps act more like advisors than stereotypical salespeople.

"However, when applied in an HR context, it's more about facilitating problem-solving discussions within the team rather than directly selling a solution. It's about adopting a collaborative approach to address business challenges. As an HR professional, you're essentially acting as an internal consultant to your team or organization.

"You aim to ask the right questions to uncover underlying issues and gather insights that lead to practical solutions. Instead of imposing predefined solutions, you guide the discussion and encourage people to share their perspectives."

I like the sound of this. "Go on," I urge her.

She continues. "For example, let's say a department is facing a high turnover rate. Instead of jumping to conclusions or implementing generic solutions, you would initiate conversations to understand the root causes. You might ask questions like: *What factors are contributing to employee turnover? Are there any patterns or trends that we're overlooking? How do employees feel about their work environment and growth opportunities?*

"By actively listening to the responses and encouraging open dialogue, you create a collaborative environment where team members feel empowered to contribute their ideas and insights.

"This approach fosters innovation. It also increases buy-in and commitment to the eventual solution, which will be vital to the success of your HR projects."

Wow. I'm blown away. I feel a weight being lifted from my shoulders, and I finally see how I'm going to be strategic at the planning meeting.

"Thanks for sharing that with me, Sasha! Let me double-check that I've got it.

"So, from an HR perspective, consultative selling involves leveraging my expertise to guide discussions, facilitate problem-solving, and drive consensus around actionable solutions that address real business needs?

"I won't need to 'sell' anything in the meeting. I'll be facilitating productive conversations that lead to tangible results for the organization. And that is how I will be **speaking strategically!**"

"You've got it!" she smiles. "Shall we take a few minutes to talk over the final part of your **Be Strategic** cycle? What are your thoughts about how you're going to act strategically?"

"By the way," she adds, "I'm totally happy to continue, as I have a lot of ideas about what I'm going to do after the meeting."

"Yes, please! I'd welcome the chance to get your take on my plans for how 'Strategic Luisa' will continue to act."

I explain. "First, I've found that blocking out 90 minutes per day as 'strategic thinking time' has been incredibly valuable. I'm going to devote at least one session to evaluating my own performance in the planning meeting so I can identify aspects I still need to work on, and then I'll block out time to do this.

"I'll prepare for upcoming meetings by thinking through the strategic questions to ask. I'll also anticipate the contribution HR will make to achieving the strategic business plan."

"That's a great habit to get into," Sasha responds affirmingly. "A daily moment of reflection allows you to switch from your own daily thinking to a big-picture perspective. Like a hawk or an eagle, it starts on the ground and can see whatever is close. As it soars higher, it can see for miles—it sees the world, even movements in the distance that don't seem significant right now."

I get excited. "Yes! That's exactly the analogy the conference speaker used! I love it. I get that I need to be agile and see the long-term view, far in the distance, while not losing sight of today's challenges."

"It's a great analogy. And do you have some ideas about how you'll continue to work strategically with your peers? How will you maintain your position as a thought leader?" Sasha asks.

"Well, I hope that after the meeting, they'll have more respect for me and understand how HR can work as their business partner to help them achieve their objectives."

Sasha is thoughtful. She seems to need more convincing that it will be enough.

"Does anyone in your company engage in scenario planning exercises?" she asks.

This is another thing I'd never heard of. "Not to my knowledge," I reply.

"Scenario planning is a powerful tool for anticipating future developments and preparing a team to navigate various possible situations effectively."

"Can you explain how it works in practice?" I ask.

"Sure. First, it's a collaborative exercise. Engage your team—the executive team—in brainstorming sessions where they can collectively identify key trends, uncertainties, and potential disruptions relevant to your organization or industry. These could involve analyzing market trends, technological advancements, regulatory changes, or shifts in consumer behavior.

"Once you've identified these key factors," she continues, "you guide the team in developing a range of scenarios that depict different potential futures based on varying combinations of these factors. During this process, encourage creativity and out-of-the-box thinking to explore optimistic and pessimistic scenarios.

"Once you've collectively outlines these scenarios, you can facilitate discussions to assess each scenario's potential impact on your organization. You'll encourage your peers to consider how each scenario would affect different aspects of the business."

I'm eating this up, and I eagerly urge her to continue.

"From there, you'll all collaborate to formulate strategies and action plans tailored to each scenario. You'll help identify measures that you can take to capitalize on opportunities presented by favorable scenarios and mitigate risks associated with less desirable outcomes.

"Finally, it's essential to monitor and adjust as the situation evolves.

"Scenario planning isn't a one-time exercise. Instead, it's a continuous process of anticipating, preparing for, and adapting to change.

"By leading scenario planning exercises in this manner, you'll empower your team to think strategically, anticipate challenges, and proactively position your organization for success in an uncertain future."

I'm awed by the possibilities but somehow feel reticent. "That sounds amazing, but I'm not sure I'd be ready to jump in and facilitate right away. I think I'd like to see one of these sessions in action before trying to run one."

"Well, it's likely that I'll be involved in scenario planning as part of the strategy meeting. You should definitely be there to see how it works. Observe the first time, and then after that, you'll be ready to facilitate independently."

"That would be awesome! Wow, you've been amazing, Sasha! I feel much clearer now. But before you go, I have one more question for you."

"In your experience, what are the kinds of roadblocks that can derail the transition from transactional to transformational HR? How can I avoid the pitfalls and stay on the path of **being** strategic?" I ask.

"Well, the first thing I want to say is that based on our conversation today, you've got this, Luisa! You comprehend the need to understand the business landscape, embrace a growth mindset, and seek opportunities to develop new skills.

"But if you're asking me, you need to keep a few things in mind to make sure you don't get stuck by common blockers that can prevent HR professionals from focusing on strategy.

"First, it's essential to *avoid daily whirlwinds*—those situations that demand your immediate attention. It's tempting to focus on them because there's an immediate payoff when you resolve them—a rush of endorphins when calm is restored and everyone's happy again—until next time, of course."

I nod knowingly. "Yes, I get that. I'll have to make sure that I delegate our whirlwinds to my HR Specialist."

She agrees. "Next. Never employ the 'I'm not good with numbers' excuse. *Never.* You're part of a business, you want to be taken seriously, and that requires an understanding of the bottom line. You don't have to be a math genius, but start where you are and *embrace the numbers*. Or stay where you are. You said it earlier. No other function would promote a person to a senior position if they claimed 'I'm not good with numbers'."

She is so right. "That's so true! If I want respect from the business leaders around me, I'd better start talking in their language. HR is going to have to become much more focused on finance. I have to admit, though, while I 100% agree with you, it's a bit intimidating."

Sasha knows how to reassure me. "Of course it is. This is a new way of thinking for you, but you have a growth mindset, so think—how can you make it work?"

I think for a moment. "I guess I don't have to know it all from Day One. I can reach out to colleagues and learn from other subject matter experts."

"Of course, you've got it! You'll be surprised by how much people will be willing to help you—especially if they're the kind of people who love finance!"

I'm excited. This talk with Sasha has helped clear away my confusion and given me the confidence boost I need as I prepare for the strategy planning meeting.

After graciously accepting my thanks and appreciation for all her help, Sasha heads off to her next meeting, and I head back to the office, my head buzzing with new ideas. Finance, questioning, consultative selling, scenario planning—there's so much to learn as I continue my journey of thinking, speaking, and acting strategically! *Instead of being intimidated, I can't wait to get started.*

Reflections for the Reader

1. THINK

- ✓ How do I define "value" in HR terms?
- ✓ How easily do I get distracted by "low-hanging fruit" — situations I can resolve immediately or that require little-to-no effort? How rewarding are they for me?
- ✓ Do I calculate ROI (Return on Investment) when proposing HR initiatives? How willing am I to engage in constructive conversations about ROI and the bottom line? How do I engage with financial topics in general?

2. SPEAK

- ✓ Do I leverage my network to help me grow and develop?
- ✓ How effective am I as a facilitator in meetings with my peers? Am I acting as a business partner and guiding them to explore and find practical solutions?

3. ACT

- ✓ Do I carry out "scenario planning" exercises with my peers or my team? What would be the benefits? What is stopping me?

CHAPTER

10

THE ADVENTURE BEGINS

I'm here to build something for the long-term. Anything else is a distraction.

— *Mark Zuckerberg, Founder of Facebook*

Danielle presents her HR Strategic Plan and departmental restructuring to the C-suite

The COO has approved my plan. I've shared it with my team, and they're excited by the changes in their roles.

The next opportunity is to gain the support of the CEO and my colleagues on the executive team. I'm presenting it at an upcoming meeting that includes the heads of the manufacturing and logistics units.

They have allocated me a 30-minute slot to present the changes, but I requested more time. I've transformed my department, so this isn't something to rush through.

I know I have to grab their attention and make clear "what's in it for them" if they're going to support our new strategic approach. And it will take time and space to address their questions and concerns.

I receive a note that my slot is now a full 60 minutes.

I've prepared, revised, and rehearsed. This is a real test of my ability to speak and act strategically. I need to get it right the first time.

The day of the meeting arrives. I open the meeting by thanking my peers for being so generous with their time when I've met with them individually over the past few weeks and for sharing their concerns about HR so openly. I begin by addressing the basics: why HR is a critical part of the organization and what contribution we make to the company's success.

"Do we all agree that to achieve our overarching aim, we have to leverage three assets?" I ask. "*Financially*, we must generate money and invest it wisely. Our *physical assets* are our facilities, our "hardware," our products. And the final asset is our people. These are the three pillars of our organizational success."

SLIDE 1

HR as Strategic Partner for "People"

✓ How do we choose people?
✓ How can we invest in their growth?
✓ How can we set our people up for success in meeting company goals?

Though a bit nervous, I channel the energy, and I'm feeling confident as I launch into my presentation. "These are the fundamental questions we need to address as we move forward. As I listened to each of you, I realized that we in Human Resources have been operating in a way that perhaps worked for the business a few years ago. But since WMT's overarching aim is to drive excellence and growth, our old way of work no longer aligns with our company's needs going forward.

"So, the whole HR team has been working on rethinking everything about our work over the past couple of weeks. We want to make sure we can give each of your departments all the support you need to achieve your business unit objectives this year—and the objectives in WMT's strategic plan over the next three years.

"As I'm going to demonstrate, HR is going to become a strategic partner for We Make Things. We can leverage our greatest assets—our people. The company needs a new approach to Human Resources— one that's fit for the excellence and growth we're aiming for.

"So today, I'm going to present the new HR plan and introduce you to a new team structure that will transform the way we work. I'll answer all your questions at the end, but as I go through, if there's anything that's not clear, please feel free to ask."

I start with the title slide, which clarifies that our thinking is about the "big picture."

SLIDE 2

Strategic Alignment: Partnering with the Business to Elevate Excellence & Growth

I move straight into the company plan.

"People are fundamental to achieving our business goals. HR is going to play a pivotal role in driving and achieving all five strategic objectives. As we all know, these are the ones listed on the screen.

SLIDE 3

HR's 5 Key Contributions to Organizational Excellence and Growth

- ✓ Achieve a 25% Increase in Market Share
- ✓ Attract and Retain Top Talent
- ✓ Improve Employee Experience and Boost eNPS
- ✓ Leverage Technology for Manufacturing Excellence
- ✓ Enhance Efficiency and Achieve Cost Reduction

The VP of Sales is the first to speak up. "The increase in market share. How would the work of HR, realistically speaking, impact that?"

My response is ready. "Good question! Thank you for asking. The 25% goal is an incredibly ambitious target that will require every department in the company to be at the top of their game. WTM needs to attract top talent, and we need to stop losing our best people. So, through *acquiring talent, ensuring they have the right rewards, leveraging their skills, keeping them motivated—and, critically, ensuring that we have exceptionally skilled leaders*—HR can have a positive impact by on all of those areas."

He nods and scribbles some notes.

Next, the head of one of our most profitable production centers says, "This looks good, Danielle. But, fourth point, what does HR really have to do with 'manufacturing excellence'?"

I smile and exude knowledge and professionalism. "Thank you, Roger. Currently, training is necessary to address the gaps we have today. It addresses the things that slow us down. With technology evolving so rapidly, and to stay ahead of our competitors, we're going to have to face the future and plan to train for tomorrow's world.

"Our team will work with you to anticipate what type of training your team is going to need to stay current and maintain manufacturing excellence. And then we'll ensure the right level of training and support for your WMT employees so they can adapt effectively to technological advances. We're going to train for excellence."

"OK, sounds good—but how will you organize that?" another manager asks.

Still smiling, I respond, "Stay with me, Dave, and I'll be getting to that." *I don't feel great brushing him off, but I can't afford to get derailed.*

However, before I can move on, our VP of Finance needs me to clarify the fifth bullet, which focuses on enhancing efficiency and achieving cost reduction.

I explain. "Yes, thank you, Nick. Another great question. I've put two KPIs in place to make sure we target this objective and measure our progress. The first is to achieve a 10% cost reduction in HR processes year over year. The second, tied to our bottom line, is to improve the HR cost-to-revenue ratio by 5% over the next fiscal year.

"I'm confident we can achieve those goals mainly by leveraging technology and implementing cost-effective talent acquisition and development strategies."

I suspect he's not going to accept that vague answer. Nope. He asks, "Specifically, what kind of cost-effective talent acquisition strategies do you intend to implement? Can you give us an example?"

I'm on top of it. "Sure. One of our biggest challenges in reducing costs as well as increasing manufacturing efficiency right now is the constant churn of employees.

"Imagine that if every time a piece of valuable equipment got broken or stolen, the production units just said 'Get me a replacement quick! I don't care how much it costs, how much we paid for the one that broke, or how hard they are to get hold of.' No, a loss like that would be taken seriously and appear in the figures, right?"

I see nods around the room.

"Attrition is a heavy cost. Each time someone leaves, it impacts productivity, takes management time, and it's more expensive to find and train a replacement than many of us are aware. More than that, we're effectively training people who take off with the skills and knowledge we've provided them, often to benefit our rivals."

I see even more nods of agreement.

"You'll see that my plan includes strategies to improve the employee experience, providing career development initiatives as well as operational training. These won't come at zero cost, but they'll be cost-effective over the long term and will support the achievement of that 5th critical objective as well as the other ones."

Nick nods slowly and makes a note on his pad. Perhaps not 100% convinced, he seems to be letting it go for now.

I summarize that slide by emphasizing that HR is aligned with the business goals: "So these objectives are where HR will play a vital role in driving the company, ensuring sustainable growth and success."

I want to be sure the meeting isn't derailed, leaving me out of time to make my key points. I move swiftly to the following slides.

SLIDE 4

Now, it's time to explain the "How" of the plan.

SLIDE 5

Strategic HR Technologies

✓ Integrate advanced HR analytics platforms for data-driven decision-making and alignment with organizational goals
✓ Optimize recruitment technologies and ensure seamless integration with other HR systems for efficiency.

I step back to the podium. "To deliver our ambitious agenda, HR must transform how we work. We need to move from *transactional*—that is, efficient routine admin—to *transformational*, which involves becoming a strategic partner in helping the business achieve its goals.

"Fundamental to this change is harnessing technology. With the support of the IT team, we've identified an HR platform that will integrate and streamline every part of the employee lifecycle—from recruitment to onboarding, performance and training, and absence management to offboarding. It will be far more visible throughout the company, so managers can finally make decisions about their team without running to HR for 'approval.'"

They like that last point.

"It's also employee-facing, so employees will be able to access their personal data, request leave, and more—again eliminating the need for HR or managers to spend valuable time on routine inquiries. How many times have you been asked, 'How many days of leave days do I have left?' "When does my maternity leave end?'"

They smile in recognition.

The VP of Finance speaks up again. "It sounds good, but is it really going to save cost? These systems are expensive and take heavy IT resources to customize and implement. Then everyone needs to be retrained to use it, you realize." He sounds a bit smug and cynical.

But I've got it. "The latest cloud-based systems don't involve heavy up-front costs and can be installed within a day. There's no need for IT to be extensively involved in the installation—just to help us transfer our current data into the new system. And since we're still using Excel for a lot of our tracking, that shouldn't be too hard."

A voice pipes up. "What about data security? Can the system you want guarantee that our employee data will be safe?"

I nod. "Yes. Absolutely. Mike, our Compliance Specialist, has been working with the IT team on this, and they've given us the okay for the system we've chosen. So, here's the KPI that will measure how well we achieve this objective."

I point to the screen as I walk towards it.

SLIDE 6

HR KPI: Technology Implementation and Efficiency:

Achieve a 10% increase year on year in HR process efficiency through technology adoption.

"Let me move on, and I'll keep returning with details about how we'll be using the system to transform the way we work as I go through the objectives of the HR 3-Year Strategic Plan. Let's start with Talent Acquisition and Retention."

SLIDE 7

Talent Acquisition and Retention

✓ Develop comprehensive talent acquisition strategies aligned with organizational growth objectives.
✓ Utilize cutting-edge recruitment technologies and data-driven processes for efficient talent sourcing and screening.
✓ Enhance employer branding initiatives to position the organization as an employer of choice and showcase a positive workplace culture.

"I think you'll all agree that we're lucky to have Lauren looking after talent acquisition: she's a competent and experienced professional. But how many of you would welcome a shorter time-to-hire cycle?"

Many heads nod.

"With our new platform, Lauren's time will be freed from updating trackers, answering queries about hiring progress, and scheduling interviews. Instead, she'll work with the departments on manpower planning and ensuring that the right people are in place when and where they are needed.

"She'll leverage the features of the system to create ads and access candidates via social media as well as traditional channels. This will reduce the amount we pay to agencies and consultants, which, this year-to-date alone, have cost us…"

I tell them how much. I hear some audible gasps. Many eyebrows rise at that figure.

"In addition to filtering applications automatically, we can integrate the latest psychometric tools to ensure that we're interviewing people with the right profile as well as the right resumé. This will reduce the time each of spends on meeting candidates who aren't

148

what the business needs. Interview scheduling will be streamlined to make your lives easier.

"And as we focus on the future, we'll be forging stronger links with local schools and colleges to raise WTM's profile as a potential employer and make it easier to source and develop entry-level employees with a tech-apprenticeship program and a graduate fast-track program. That will help us reach the company's goals in terms of growth and manufacturing excellence and enhance our reputation as an employer of choice.

"Here are the KPIs we've set for this objective." I change the slide, and all eyes turn to the screen.

SLIDE 8

HR KPI: Talent Acquisition and Retention

✓ Achieve an employee retention rate of 80% over the next year.
✓ Achieve a 30% reduction in time-to-fill critical positions through advanced recruitment technologies.

This causes a ripple of interest.

A cynical voice in the back asks, "So, HR is going to make sure our employees stop resigning, then?" The group chuckles, but I'm unfazed.

"No, sadly, we can't do that—we can't make everyone in the company happy, and actually, that's not our role. As business leaders, all of you still need to look after your people. What we will be doing in HR is recruiting smarter, so we know that the people we're onboarding are the right fit for WMT. We'll also be implementing strategies to increase engagement, which brings me to my next objective."

SLIDE 9

Employee Experience and Engagement

✓ Track and improve eNPS through regular employee feedback sessions and data analytics.
✓ Utilize digital tools for real-time communication, collaboration, and professional development opportunities.
✓ Implement initiatives to enhance workplace satisfaction, well-being, and engagement.

I continue. "We already conduct the annual employee survey and get the eNPS score, but what have we been doing with it? In truth, very little. My plan ensures that we focus on leveraging the feedback data to create strategies that will improve it. The new HR platform will feature a more user-friendly survey experience and analyze the data, breaking it down accurately so that we can identify our employees' pain points and address them.

"That's why our KPIs for this objective are ambitious, but working in partnership with all of your departments, we believe they're achievable."

SLIDE 10

HR KPI: Employee Experience and eNPS

✓ Improve eNPS by 10 points year over year.
✓ Enhance overall employee satisfaction through the utilization of digital communication and collaboration tools.

I read the KPIs on this slide about improving employee experience. This also seems to be well-received by the audience.

The VP of Research & Development asks, "How are you going to address the second KPI?"

I explain. "Again, with our new platform, we'll launch a company social media platform for all employees, making it easier and faster to communicate about work. This will help to break down the silos that build up between departments.

"And in the social chat space, in addition to private chats, we'll have group forums to discuss topics of concern to everyone. That way, we'll be able to take the temperature, so to speak, and understand the mood and concerns of our employees in real time—and respond to them.

"One thing that we already know is on our employees' minds is the lack of structured development we offer. So, a strategic response from HR will be necessary over the coming year. We'll need to work closely with the entire company since our next objective is *providing development opportunities and upskilling for the future.*

SLIDE #11

Providing Development Opportunities/ Upskilling for the Future

- ✓ Identify skill gaps through regular assessments and provide targeted training and development opportunities.
- ✓ Foster a culture of continuous learning to prepare employees for the future of work.
- ✓ Develop a framework for upskilling employees in emerging technologies and future-oriented skills.
- ✓ Implement mentorship and coaching programs to support employee growth and readiness for evolving roles.

The points on this slide look good, but I'm not going to let them fall under the heading of 'nice-to-have,' so I plan to follow with the KPIs.

Before I can get there, the head of our most recently opened manufacturing site has a very practical concern. "Okay, we've got the part about training being needed, but who's going to work with us to identify these skill gaps, create the development plans for each employee, and deliver the training for the future? We've already got enough on our plate delivering what the business needs today!"

I'm glad she's picked up on this because, inadvertently, she's making the case for the new role I'm creating. I reply, "I think we all agree that it's time to get serious about the way we train our employees to meet the current and the future needs of the business. Am I right?"

Everyone agrees.

"And we agree that this is absolutely fundamental to our growth and that excellence needs to be addressed on a company-wide level, rather than by individual business units?"

They're with me so far—perhaps because they don't want this extra responsibility to distract from their own objectives.

"Okay, that will require financial as well as human resources. Right now, planning and organizing all of this is a pressure for you. Our employees don't feel they're being developed or looked after properly, and we're already paying the price.

"Training will remain a departmental responsibility since HR can't achieve these objectives in isolation. Of course, you managers will need to be involved, and we will need your full support to drive company-wide training and development initiatives.

"As VP of HR, it's my role to ensure that we provide the resources you need for support and partner with you to deliver what is required: not just today but into the future.

"Training underpins all our goals. Only when we're sure our employees have the skills to achieve them can we set meaningful goals based on WTM's strategic plan. So these are our KPIs for this HR objective." I change the slide to project the KPIs.

SLIDE 12

HR KPIs: Providing Development Opportunities/ Upskilling for the Future

Company Training Needs Analysis

✓ KPI: Ensure a 12-month company training plan is in place, based on a comprehensive TNA in each department/business unit.

Employee Engagement in Development Programs:

✓ KPI: 80% of employees have an Individual Development Plan aligned with the company's business objectives for the year.

Coaching and Mentorship Program

✓ KPI: 75% of WMT leaders trained as coaches.
✓ KPI: 20 volunteers trained and certified as mentors.

The COO asks me to clarify. "So Danielle, who's going to create these Individual Development Plans, and whose responsibility are they?"

"Great question," I reply, "and I'm glad for the opportunity to be specific about this at this point. Individual Development Plans are a powerful way to ensure that our employees feel they are not only being trained for today's tasks but also being stretched to achieve their full potential as they prepare for future roles. Obviously, *IDPs need to be owned by the company, co-created by each leader and their team members, then facilitated and tracked by HR.*"

I don't feel a massive surge of enthusiasm for this answer. I'm about to move on when our Head of Marketing has a question.

"About the coaching and mentorship programs. Who's eligible to volunteer for the mentorship program?"

I respond with an effort to arouse enthusiasm. "Well, naturally we want our senior people to volunteer and help to guide and develop the next generation. But there's no reason why junior team members who've shown leadership potential shouldn't be recognized with an invitation to the program. The KPI of lining up 20 mentors is only for the first year. We envisage that this will be an ongoing initiative."

She seems happy with that.

But I'm feeling some resistance starting to build up from the group. Perhaps there's a concern that the Strategic HR Plan will make life easier for HR while putting more responsibility on their shoulders. It's time to address this.

"I hope I've explained how this HR strategic plan aligns with the organization's overarching goal, emphasizing the role of HR technologies, talent management, and employee experience, achieving organizational excellence and sustainable growth.

"A plan is one thing. Now we have to deliver it, and I want to make clear right now that it's my aim to deliver all these objectives without needing you to take your eye off the ball in your own areas.

"That's why I've restructured the HR department and created a team that's fit for the future. This team can give you the support you need and help We Make Things achieve the 3-Year Strategic Plan's goals and objectives."

SLIDE 13

New HR Department Structure - Fit for the Future

Current	New Strategic Focus
VP HR	VP HR
Talent Acquisition & Retention Specialist	Talent Acquisition Manager
Compensation & Benefits Specialist	Compensation & Benefits Specialist
Employee Relations & Compliance Specialist	Employee Engagement & Experience Specialist
HR Generalist/Coordinator	HR Operations Specialist
	Training and Development Manager

I pause for a few seconds to allow them to review the changes. Then, I take each role in turn, reviewing the key points from their revised role description to make sure I highlight the new strategic focus of each role.

"Let's start with the Talent Acquisition Manager."

SLIDE 14

Talent Acquisition Manager

Strategic Focus

- ✓ Develop a Comprehensive Talent Acquisition Plan.
- ✓ Align talent acquisition strategies with the organizational goal of attracting top talent for increased market share.
- ✓ Minimize agency recruitment spending by using digital channels for targeted employer branding initiatives.
- ✓ Leverage the HR platform to enhance the employer brand and attract high-caliber professionals with reduced time-to-hire.

We've already discussed these aspects in some detail, so I move on once I've checked that there are no questions.

"Next, we come to a very important position, the Compensation and Benefits Specialist."

SLIDE 15

Compensation and Benefits Specialist

Strategic Focus

- ✓ Design and manage the organization's compensation structure.
- ✓ Align compensation strategies with the organization's overarching goal of excellence and growth.
- ✓ Analyze market trends to recommend updated compensation structures and benefits programs to remain competitive.

"Until now," I explain, the HR Compensation and Benefits Specialist has spent the vast majority of his time on routine tasks, monitoring the headcount and budget, and answering employee queries.

"From now, he'll have a more strategic focus—ensuring that our compensation structure is not only working today but that it will act as a pull-factor for the best talent in the market, while of course, being aligned with company performance. As a result, he'll not only be working closely with the Talent Acquisition Manager but partnering with our leaders in the business to optimize their headcount and payroll budget.

The VP of Finance adds, "We've definitely been missing a systematic and data-driven approach to C&B—compensation and benefits. I'm sure your new IT platform will have a module that makes analysis easier, but my team will be ready to offer any support you need."

"I appreciate that offer, Nick! We're looking forward to working closely with your team and, in fact, all our stakeholders, to create a market-leading C&B offer that will enhance our brand going forward while aligning with the financial realities we're facing now and in future."

I turn back toward the screen. "The next role is the Employee Experience and Engagement Specialist."

SLIDE 16

Employee Experience and Engagement Specialist

Strategic Focus

✓ Utilize employee feedback and HR analytics to drive initiatives that enhance workplace satisfaction, well-being, and engagement.

✓ Manage employee performance review process, using IT to align individual employee evaluations with the organization's strategic plan.

Perhaps, despite the newly future-facing nature, this role is more clearly identifiable with traditional HR activities, so there are no challenges. Moving on, I introduce the role of the HR Operations Specialist.

SLIDE 17

HR Operations Specialist

Strategic Focus

- ✓ Implement lean and agile methodologies for efficient HR operations.
- ✓ Streamline onboarding, offboarding, and attendance management through technology-driven solutions.
- ✓ Conduct research and ensure legal compliance in all processes.

"This role has previously been 100% transactional and admin-focused. The new platform will streamline our processes and dramatically reduce the time spent on routine queries. So, the person in this role will now focus on key points in the employee journey to enhance our employer brand."

Overall, the mood in the room seems optimistic. Before I can continue, the VP of Sales asks: "So who is responsible for the coaching program, the individual development plans, the mentoring, the training for the future, and all the rest of the good stuff you're promising?"

I couldn't have asked for a better introduction to the new role!

"Great question! As I've already mentioned, and I think you all agree, to implement all those development initiatives, we need resources, human as well as financial. That's why I've created a new role at We Make Things: our first-ever Talent Development Manager."

SLIDE 18

Talent Development Manager Role

Create Strategic Planning

✓ A comprehensive talent development strategy focusing on upskilling and reskilling employees to meet future business needs.
✓ Collaborate with cross-functional teams, including HR, operations, and leadership, to identify training needs based on performance gaps and strategic objectives.

Collaboration and Stakeholder Engagement

✓ Engage with external training providers, industry associations, and educational institutions to leverage external expertise and resources.

✓ Drive a culture of continuous learning and improvement within the organization by fostering an environment that values and encourages personal and professional development.

Leadership Development

✓ Design leadership development programs to nurture and develop future leaders within the organization.
✓ Provide coaching and mentorship opportunities to high-potential employees to support their career advancement and the succession plan.

I click to put up a second slide as I walk them through the various elements in the job description.

SLIDE 19

Talent Development Manager Role contd.

Technology Integration

- ✓ Leverage technology platform (LMS) to facilitate learning and development initiatives, content delivery, and tracking.
- ✓ Explore emerging technologies such as virtual reality (VR) and augmented reality (AR) to enhance training experiences and outcomes.

Measurement and Evaluation

- ✓ Establish metrics and KPIs to measure the effectiveness of training programs, including employee engagement, performance improvement, and return on investment (ROI).

The COO chimes in to add support. "This is a major new role on the HR team and one that's going to be vital in driving WTM forward to achieve our plan."

And the team agrees.

I've done it! I've gained their buy-in for the HR Strategic Plan and for the team structure I'll need to support it.

But they're not ready to let me get off that easily.

Nick, the VP of Finance, speaks up again. "Danielle, I think your plan is very well thought out. But you know that, across the business, we're asking for cuts in cost, and that involves sacrifices everywhere. You've just added a fairly senior role to your team, which will increase the HR payroll substantially. Isn't there a danger that this will seem like another example of HR being out of sync with the rest of us?"

I've prepared for this question. "You know, Nick, I've thought long and hard about that. Originally, I was considering cutting one of my team and sharing their tasks among the rest. But I realized that this is exactly what would keep us out of sync with the business—carrying on in the same old way and at reduced capacity.

"That's why I started looking at the HR function strategically. I went back to the drawing board and reimagined how we'd need to be organized to contribute effectively to drive the company forward to achieve the goals of the 3-Year Strategic Plan.

"From there, I created the HR Plan—and a team capable of delivering it."

He counters. "Oh, I understand. I'm not trying to take any of that away from you. I get what you're aiming for. But still, I'm not convinced that you'll not be increasing the cost."

I'm ready with my analysis. "As I've already mentioned, the new IT system will not only help us become far less reliant on recruitment agencies and consultants but will also open up new, cost-effective sourcing channels via social media.

"When we consider the emphasis on training and development that the company's strategic plan requires, designing and delivering in-house solutions will allow us to *drastically reduce our spending on ad-hoc external programs*, which have been very costly for us. Last year, in fact, these external costs were..."

I tell them how much, and suddenly, they're all paying attention again.

I continue. "And when we consider intangible savings such as *reduction in wasted management time in interviews, enhanced employer branding, and more,* I can justify the reorganization, and the new roles, as being cost effective as well as contributing to ‹excellence and growth'."

I need to seal this deal.

"And as I said earlier, to meet my KPIs, I need to achieve a cost reduction of 10% in HR processes year over year and to improve the HR cost-to-revenue ratio by 5% over the next fiscal year. *I'm ready to be measured on those.*"

I've made my point. I pause to let it sink in. I hear whispers as they turn to talk to each other about some of my points.

Then I bring things back to order as I continue. "Just before we close, I'd like to share details of my new strategic focus with you. So, here's the new VP of HR role description, which I think encapsulates the new direction of HR and its alignment with WTM's strategy."

SLIDE 20

VP HR (Strategic Leadership)

Responsibilities:

- ✓ Provide strategic leadership to align the HR team and initiatives with the overarching goal of organizational excellence and growth.
- ✓ Develop and communicate a clear vision for HR's role in achieving increased market share, top talent attraction, improved employee experience, leveraged technology, enhanced efficiency, and achieved cost reduction.

- ✓ Lead the development of a high-performing team by cultivating an understanding of the business and facilitating strategic and tactical skills to achieve organizational objectives.
- ✓ Oversee the development and execution of HR strategies to support organizational goals.

I invite their questions, but none come. Instead, the leaders express their support for the changes, which they tell me are long overdue. They're looking forward to welcoming my team and working together.

I end the meeting on a high. I've achieved my goal—the HR plan is now in place, and it's up to me to act strategically to ensure it's delivered.

Returning to my office, the whole HR team is there, waiting in anticipation.

I exclaim, "They loved it, and we've got the green light to get to work!"

The office bursts out in applause. We take a few more moments to celebrate our success—and why not? I'm going to ask them to put in a lot of hard work over the coming months to deliver what I've promised.

"I really need to thank you all for your hard work and the ideas you've put in to create our HR strategic plan. You should feel proud of what we achieved in such a short time."

They do, and we take a little more time to share how good we're feeling. They even thank me for giving them the opportunity to stretch themselves and discover a new way of working.

"So now," I say, "we've got to deliver! Looking at your new role description. Linking it to the HR plan, I want each of you to come up with your goals for next year, and then we'll divide them into 3-, 6-, 9-, and 12-month milestones.

"And Lauren, as a priority, you have three months to find the right professional to fill that Talent Development position and become the latest addition to our fantastic, strategic HR team."

And there we are. That's it for today. I head home, still buzzing from my presentation. My partner wants to tell me what he's planned for our upcoming vacation. My mom calls to catch up and tell me about the daughter of one of her friends who got engaged, got married, and had a baby within ten months. Or, who knows, maybe landed on Mars.

I listen patiently to everything, glowing with satisfaction about my day and thinking about how I'm going to have a lot to tell Luisa and Sam next time we meet—and how I'm going to create a new future for HR, starting tomorrow, that makes a tangible contribution to achieving my company's goals for the future.

Reflections for the Reader

1. THINK

- ✓ Is the current structure of my HR team fit for its purpose? How could I adjust roles to ensure that they align with the strategic plan?
- ✓ How aware am I of developments in HR technology? Are we leveraging technology effectively to increase efficiency and achieve our objectives?
- ✓ How do we approach training and development across the company? Is it "owned" by the whole company or seen as solely the responsibility of HR?

2. SPEAK

- ✓ How proactive am I in presenting strategic HR initiatives and progress at meetings with my peers? How effective are my presentations?
- ✓ How do I celebrate success with my HR team? How do I communicate our success to the wider company?

3. ACT

- ✓ The strategic HR plan is in place. How am I helping my team with the creation of a manpower plan, a succession plan, and a training and development plan?

CHAPTER

11

THE
TRANSFORMATIONAL
CHAMPION

*Great things in business are never done
by one person; they're done by a team of
people.*

— Steve Jobs

Sam teams up with his CEO to present the need for a Strategic Plan

As the hologram fades and the applause from the team dies down, I catch the CEO's eye. He's pleased that his plan has worked, and he's ready to take the floor.

First, let me track back a few days. While I'd been working away on my presentation, I'd had a vague awareness that he was going to do something big, something nobody was expecting. But he'd been uncharacteristically secretive about whatever he was planning, and despite my hints, I couldn't get him to confide in me.

On the morning of the meeting, a team of technicians I've never seen before starts setting up the conference room behind locked doors.

When the leadership team drifts in after lunch and takes their seats around the conference table, they're not exactly pumped. Some from the remote sites are joining us via video links.

As the automatic blinds close and plunge the room into darkness, the CEO addresses his team. "First, I'd like to thank you all for coming. It's a big day. We're at a turning point in the history of WAT. We have a lot to get done and, in a while, Sam's going to lead you through it."

The VP of Sales speaks up. "Awesome, but do we know how long this is going to take? It's just that I have…"

The CEO cuts him off. "Got it, Brad. We're all busy. But as I've said, today, we're changing the game. So, if any of you have anything scheduled for the rest of the day, cancel it now."

He pauses while people pick up their phones and do what they've been told.

"We'll get down to work soon. But before that, I want to introduce you to a very special guest, my buddy, Dexter…"

His buddy just happens to be Dexter Steele—host of the The Art of Oops podcast with an average of 6.6 million listeners per episode. He's one of the world's top five business gurus, with 4.5 million followers on Instagram and over 2 million YouTube subscribers. He's also an author with 28 weeks at #1 in the NYT Bestsellers list with his latest tome: *Why Winning Start-Ups Win—Strategic Hacks to Rocket-Fuel Your Success.*

But Dexter's not physically in the room because he's in Hong Kong right now in the middle of another of his record-breaking world tours. Instead, he joins us by hologram, solving the mystery of what that technical team has been setting up with such secrecy.

How exactly does Dexter come to be in our first strategy meeting? I learned later that our CEO, who'd previously been a guest on one of Dexter's four-hour podcasts (17.1 million views), had decided to call in a favor.

The WAT team is in awe. We're in the presence of a global celebrity, and Dexter doesn't disappoint. He delivers a 10-minute monologue on strategy that's so motivational and inspiring that I swear some of the guys are tearing up. He ends by gifting a hard copy of his book to each person in the room.

While the team applauds in astonishment at what they've just witnessed, his image dissolves in front of us. The lights go on, and the blinds go up. The energy in the room is electric.

Now, our CEO takes center stage. He warms up slowly, taking his time, talking nostalgically about the company's early days: how fearless they all were, how ready to take on and change the world. He acknowledges the contribution of several of the people around the table and tells a few "war stories" that make everyone smile as they remember how it was back then.

He describes how the company has evolved and grown so rapidly, with one victory after another. How they've outplayed the competition and fought off hostile takeovers. How the WAT brand has become a byword for innovation. He's being totally authentic when he talks about how proud he is of what they've achieved together.

He owns the room.

Finally, he reaches today, and his tone changes as he talks about the future—speaking strategically. He introduces his ambitions for an IPO to get the investment that will catapult the company onto the global stage. Then, he makes it clear that while this will be an incredible adventure, it will also be a challenge and will place new demands on us as individuals as well as on the company. He quotes Spider-Man (what else did I expect?).

He talks about his respect for the team and his pride in what they've already achieved together. Then, he ends by explaining how he's realized that his job, as Founder and CEO, is to define the future they're going to create together.

This is what led him to think deeply about how to articulate his vision for the company—generously acknowledging the small part I'd played. He reveals a slide that, he says, encompasses his vision for the future—the reason we exist as a company, our North Star to guide us.

We Automate Things

VISION STATEMENT

To pioneer transformative SaaS solutions that redefine industries, empower individuals, and inspire global progress. To create a future where innovation knows no bounds, shaping a world of boundless possibilities and sustainable impact.

So, there it is, as he promised. And although it's a bit longer than I'd expected, he fit everything in.

He follows up with another slide:

We Automate Things

MISSION #1

To prepare the company for a successful IPO launch within 24 months.

Finally, our mission is clear.

The team is silent. Then, one by one, they express their support. They love it.

He's pleased but won't let it go with some flattery and easy promises.

"We're not going to achieve all this by accident. Starting today, we need to come together and think about everything we do in terms of whether it is moving us faster toward our #1 mission or slowing us down. Is it taking us closer or moving us in a different direction?

"A clear plan is the best way to align us and move forward. Each one of us will have a part to play in achieving it.

"That's why I made the right decision when I hired Sam as our CHRO. With his background in military service, he's the right guy to guide us. So now, over to you, Sam..."

It's my turn to step up to the podium and "sell" the concept of a strategic plan, to paint a clear picture of the advantages for my peers and the company. It's time to speak strategically.

I start by articulating the benefits.

"With a strategic plan, we'll all know what we're trying to achieve and understand the steps we each need to take.

"The priorities will be clear, and we can all focus our teams on what matters to the business and what moves us closer to our goal.

"No more working in silos. We'll be able to enlist our colleagues in other functions to support us because, in the end, we'll all be aligned with the same aim."

The room is silent and attentive, but the excitement that Dexter and the CEO created is starting to fade just a little. *I'm not sure they're 100% with me.*

So, I decide to use HR as an example to illustrate the importance of a plan that's aligned with a strategy. I'm taking a risk by opening up, but it's time to be authentic.

"When I arrived, less than two months ago, the whole company was in the middle of budgeting. Naturally, I was asked to create the HR budget for next year.

"But my dilemma was—how could I know what to invest in to add the most value to the company? What were the priorities for HR? Bringing in new employees? Training the ones we've got? Rewarding the high performers?

"I'm not ashamed to say that, at first, I was stumped. You were all generous with your time and shared your thoughts on what you needed to solve today's problems. So, I soon got to know the current situation.

"But what still wasn't clear to me was the future—that is, defining what we as a company will need to succeed in 12 months, three years, or five years.

"For my budget, I can come up with some ballpark figures based on the past, factor in inflation, and respond to some of your pressing demands.

"But unless I know where we're aiming to get to, at least in the next 12 months, how can HR play its part in getting us there? First, we need to get clear about the future.

"And that, ladies and gentlemen, is why Jason still hasn't seen my HR budget."

That breaks the ice, and everyone, including CFO Jason, laughs in recognition.

Marsha, the VP of Marketing, speaks up first. "I'm all for creating a clear company strategy. It's not easy to come up with a marketing budget, either, when we don't know where the company is heading or when things keep changing.

"Last year, we prepared a big, expensive campaign for the VS-1590 launch, and we were practically the last to know when it was canceled. As Dexter said, if we all stick to a plan, life will become much easier, and we can use our efforts on things that matter."

She's frustrated, but I don't want this to become a discussion about the past. So, I ask the team if they all share this view.

"Up to a point," responds Paul, the VP of R&D. "But what people have always loved about working at WAT is that we're agile. If something isn't working, like the VS-1590, we pivot and do something else. Wouldn't a plan inadvertently constrain us, keeping us blindly going in the wrong direction?"

Jason, as the CFO, steps in to support the idea. "The bottom line is that the way we've been operating isn't sustainable if we want to go for a market launch that will guarantee our long-term success. Investors aren't impressed by pivoting, spontaneity, and self-expression—they want to know what we'll be spending their money on, and why—what we're trying to achieve."

I step in to reassure them. "Of course, Paul and Marsha are both right in a way. The last thing we want is to kill the culture of creativity and innovation that WAT is famous for. So, the strategic plan I'm proposing will be very high-level. It will start from where we are today and where we want to get to.

"Your freedom lies in the 'how' of getting there—the steps you take. You're the experts in your fields, so it will be up to you to define those steps. And you'll be free to refine and calibrate them as you progress."

I'm pleased that everyone is so engaged.

After some more discussion, Darren joins the conversation via video link. "So, are you going to tell us the strategy today? So we'll know where we're going? It will help us over here a lot."

"Hi, Darren," I respond. "The short answer is 'no' because today's meeting is for this team, guided by our CEO's vision, to define our five key strategic objectives for the coming twelve months.

"We have twenty people in the room and four more on video. In pairs, go out, grab a coffee, stretch your legs, find a convenient place to discuss, and be back in this room and ready to present your ideas in one hour. Remote guys, link up and form a group. Since HR needs to be part of this conversation, I'll drop in with each group from time to time."

Off they go. I float between groups, listening and asking some Socratic questions when needed. I guide the conversations but am careful not to take over—I want them to own whatever they come up with.

When the groups return, each one lists what they have identified as the company's priorities for the coming year—aligned with the #1 Mission Statement. I step in to facilitate because, naturally, some ideas are duplicated and some can be consolidated under a single heading. As the group discussion flows, the CEO joins in, giving his opinion about each point. We end with a "long list" of more than twenty or so.

Gradually, we start to coalesce our thinking around the top priorities, and we organize and focus the list to define ten overarching objectives under five headings.

Innovation and Product Development

- ✓ **Continuous enhancement and innovation of the SAAS product or service.**
- ✓ **Integration of emerging technologies such as AI, machine learning, and blockchain.**

Scalability and Infrastructure

- ✓ Building scalable infrastructure to accommodate the growing user base.
- ✓ Ensuring the SAAS platform can handle increased demand without compromising performance.

Cybersecurity and Data Privacy

- ✓ Addressing and enhancing cybersecurity measures to protect user data.
- ✓ Compliance with evolving data privacy regulations.

Customer Retention and Expansion

- ✓ Focus on customer satisfaction and retention.
- ✓ Strategies to expand the customer base and increase revenue from existing clients.

Financial Sustainability and Efficiency

- ✓ Cost optimization. Conducting a comprehensive cost analysis across departments.
- ✓ Identifying areas for cost optimization without compromising product quality or customer satisfaction.

I ask the group how they feel about these objectives, and they agree that all the key priorities are covered. Our CEO gives his assent. I can see he's pleased.

So, my final task for the meeting is to ensure that the plan progresses and that we act strategically.

"We've come a long way quickly, but the real work starts here," I say with encouragement. "Now, each of you will be putting together a more detailed plan for your function and defining the steps you're going to take to move WAT towards our #1 Mission—guided by our overall vision, of course.

"Let's start with the first one: Innovation and Product Development," I say.

"That's mine!" says Paul, VP of R&D.

"Thanks, Paul. You're right, of course—but it belongs to all of us from today. Let's have some examples. Marsha, how is Marketing going to work toward this objective?"

Marsha speaks up. "Off the top of my head, we need to improve the way we analyze feedback to get ideas of what the customers want next. What their pain points are. We need to be more on the ball about the competition and what they're coming out with. We also need to look at the way we design and manage campaigns."

"Great," I respond. "So, you've already come up with some ideas of the steps you need to take to contribute. Once you've got the details worked out, they go onto your plan.

"Let's have another example: What about HR? What does HR have to do with innovation and product development? What contribution can we make?"

"I guess by finding the best design talent and paying them enough that they'll join us," Paul says.

"Right! So we need to ensure that our compensation and benefits are on target—not in one area but across the board. Therefore, one of my key steps will be to conduct a review of how we attract and reward talent to make sure we'll keep getting the best people."

Lots of heads nod. The CEO smiles appreciatively.

"Is it clear that we all have contributions, to a greater or lesser extent, to make to each of these five objectives? That these are everyone's focus for the coming year?"

They agree. They've got it.

That's enough for one day, so I wrap things up.

"So, now, it's time for some strategic action. Each of us has one week to create a 12-month plan for our department, detailing what you're going to achieve and how you're going to achieve it. Don't forget your SMART objectives—remember what Dexter had to say about them?"

They laugh because Dexter is a megafan of SMART objectives—in fact, he practically claims to have invented them.

"When you're ready, send your plans to Josh, our Comp & Bens Manager, who'll load them into the performance management system. That way, we'll all have complete visibility of progress.

"And do we agree that we'll review the plan as a team every three months to acknowledge successes and calibrate as necessary?"

They agree.

Finally, the CEO steps up and wraps up the meeting, encouraging his team to enjoy this awesome journey we're now on. It's clear how much they respect and want to please him.

Once they've all left, he turns to me and says, "Great work, Sam. I knew I'd made the right decision to hire you."

Before I have a chance to respond, he's gone.

And I'm standing alone, with a massive weight lifted from my shoulders, a smile on my face, and a plan starting to take shape in my mind.

For the next week, the energy in HQ is off the charts. Everyone's feverishly working on their plans. So, with my team, I get down to business and play my part. My colleagues constantly call me for advice on how to make sure that their people goals are aligned with the #1 mission.

From there, I conduct a detailed study about the costs of achieving all this. I work closely with my team, my peers, and the Finance department to make sure I've got our priorities right and the budget allocated.

I'm proud of what's been achieved and eager to catch up with Luisa and Danielle to share my transformation from "stuck tactician" to "strategic enterprise leader."

The only thing I need to make my life complete right now is for my baby to let me have just one good night's sleep!

Five days later, my first-ever strategic HR plan is ready. Here it is.

12-MONTH HR STRATEGIC PLAN

Executive Summary

This plan defines HR's role in achieving the company's priorities, emphasizing creating a collaborative culture and a workforce trained for innovation. HR aligns practices with the company's Vision Statement and #1 Mission Statement, fostering an environment conducive to sustained growth and success.

This approach positions HR as an essential partner in propelling the company toward success with an agile, engaged, high-performing workforce.

Alignment with Organizational Strategic Priorities

1. **Talent Acquisition and Development**

   Recruitment Strategies

   - ✓ Align hiring needs with product development and innovation initiatives.
   - ✓ Integrate emerging technologies into recruitment processes.

   Skill Development

   - ✓ Identify essential skills for the workforce related to AI, machine learning, and blockchain.
   - ✓ Implement training programs and partnerships for skill development.

   Succession Planning

   - ✓ Develop a succession plan to ensure leadership continuity during growth phases.
   - ✓ Identify key roles critical for scalability and innovation.

2. **Employee Engagement and Satisfaction**

Feedback Mechanisms

- ✓ Implement employee surveys and focus groups to gauge satisfaction.

Recognition Programs

- ✓ Introduce recognition programs tied to successful product launches and innovation milestones.
- ✓ Acknowledge and reward employees who contribute to customer retention and expansion.

Creating a Culture of Collaboration

- ✓ Foster a collaborative environment through team-building activities.
- ✓ Implement cross-functional projects to encourage collaboration across departments.

3. **Cybersecurity and Data Privacy**

Employee Training

- ✓ Provide cybersecurity awareness training for all employees.
- ✓ Educate HR staff on data privacy regulations and compliance requirements.

HR Data Protection

- ✓ Implement secure HR systems and data encryption.
- ✓ Establish protocols for handling sensitive employee information.

4. **Talent Retention and Development**

Career Development Plans

- ✓ Work with employees to create personalized development plans.
- ✓ Offer opportunities for career growth tied to business expansion.

Retention Initiatives

- ✓ Analyze employee turnover trends and implement retention strategies.
- ✓ Align benefits and incentives with company growth and financial goals.

5. **Strategic Workforce Planning**

HR Analytics

- ✓ Assess workforce capabilities and identify gaps for strategic hiring or training.

Agile HR Practices

- ✓ Assess agile HR processes to adapt to changing organizational demands.
- ✓ Foster a culture of flexibility and innovation within the HR team.

Workforce Trained for Innovation

- ✓ Develop training programs focused on cultivating innovation skills.
- ✓ Encourage a mindset of continuous learning and adaptability among employees.

Key Performance Indicators (KPIs)

1. Time-to-fill for critical positions

2. Employee satisfaction and engagement scores

3. Training program effectiveness
4. Succession planning success rates
5. Retention rates and turnover costs

Implementation Timeline

✓ Quarterly HR milestones aligned with company-wide initiatives
✓ Continuous monitoring and adjustment based on organizational needs

Resource Allocation

✓ Budget allocation for recruitment tools, training programs, and employee recognition initiatives
✓ Assessment of HR staffing plans for expertise to support business priorities

Risk Management

✓ Identify HR-related risks in each priority area.
✓ Develop mitigation strategies for identified HR risks.

Communication Plan

✓ Internal communication to align HR initiatives with overall company goals.
✓ External communication on employer brand emphasizing innovation, collaboration, and employee development.

Continuous Improvement

✓ Regularly assess the effectiveness of HR initiatives through feedback loops.
✓ Adapt HR strategies based on workforce trends and organizational learnings.

Reflections for the Reader

1. THINK

- ✓ Do I envision myself as a strategic leader in my organization? If yes, what qualities or actions support my perception? If no, what steps will I take to grow into that role?
- ✓ When I have a clear vision of where the executive team needs to go, how do I strategically facilitate the steps to guide the team from point A to point Z?

2. SPEAK

- ✓ How do I use questioning techniques to gather important insights from leadership or teams about organizational direction?
- ✓ When communicating a new vision or direction, how do I ensure that my message resonates with and engages different stakeholders?

3. ACT

- ✓ When facilitating discussions with the executive team, how do I ensure that all voices are heard while keeping the conversation focused on achieving alignment and actionable outcomes?
- ✓ How confident am I in my skills to facilitate an executive strategic planning session and to produce a strategic plan from the discussion?

STRATEGICALLY
EVER AFTER

*I think luck falls on not just the brave
but also the ones who believe they
belong there.*

— *Novak Djokovic, athlete*

Three weeks later, the group meets again. Luisa takes up the story.

For the past week, this catch-up has been on my mind. I'm so excited to share what's happened in my world since our first meeting because so much has changed.

As I arrive at the coffee shop, Sam is already there, and Danielle comes right behind me. I can already tell that something's changed for them, too. The first time we met, we were all polite but hesitant and perhaps slightly embarrassed to confide in others about our situations.

Today, though, there's a fundamental shift in energy. I'm unsure how I can tell—perhaps our body language, the broad and authentic way we smile as we greet each other.

We settle down with our coffee and get ready to start the conversation. I make a suggestion. "I don't know how you both feel, but so much has changed for me since the last meeting, and it's all related to the Think-Speak-Act model. Rather than explore our challenges today, I'd like to take this time to celebrate our successes."

They agree with this approach.

Danielle begins. "Why don't you start, Luisa? And what's gone well for you? Have you been thinking more strategically? "

I respond eagerly. "Yes, I've been trying to do that in every aspect of my work. But if you remember, my most pressing issue was to make the right impact in the strategy planning meeting.

"Once I got back to work after the conference, the first thing I needed to do was give myself time to think. So, I blocked my calendar, scheduled meetings more efficiently, and delegated routine tasks to my HR Specialist."

Sam asks, "And how did that go?"

"It really helped me focus. Preparation was going to be essential for my personal rebrand in the strategy meeting. I had to get serious and understand the business and the external challenges we were going to face. Research needs time and focus."

Danielle gets it. "You're so right, Luisa. I'd been making the same mistake, staying busy with everyday tasks. One of the things I've been doing over the past three weeks is reviewing all my notes from my MBA so I can now put the theory I learned into action. And I've been listening to podcasts with the big thought leaders on strategy. I don't know if you've heard of Dexter Steele—he's now my go-to guy."

Sam is typically a great listener, but he seems to be trying hard not to choke on his coffee through his laugh. "Great story," he says with a grin. "I'll tell you later."

Then he turns to me. "So, Luisa, you took very practical steps to help yourself think strategically? Making it a priority to prepare for meetings is fundamental."

We agree that it is. He continues, "And how else has your thinking changed to a future focus, Luisa?"

"Well, before the conference," I reply, "I was convinced I should have all the solutions—and I didn't have any! Now, I've changed my mindset. I make sure that every conversation with the leadership team at WFT is future-focused. Yes, we talk about the past and the situation today, but I always ask how people envision the value they will add to the future of the business, the steps we'll need to get to our goal, or the business problems we'll need to solve.

"With practice, I'm getting much better at asking strategic questions.

"And when I met up with Sasha McConnell, our strategy consultant, she consolidated everything for me. When thinking strategically before committing to any HR initiative, the question becomes: *Does it align with and add value to our direction? Does it contribute to the achievement of our vision?*"

Sam and Danielle nod in agreement.

"Another point she was crystal clear about is this: *As HR professionals, we don't have the luxury of being the only part of the business to ignore finance.* If we want to be considered as a business partner, if we want to add value and contribute to the bottom line, we have to get a grip on the numbers. That was a lesson I needed to hear."

"That is so true," agrees Danielle. "How can we be credible as business partners or internal consultants if we don't understand the financial realities?"

Sam summarizes. "So that's two more aspects of thinking strategically: aligning HR initiatives with business objectives and making financial aspects a key consideration."

He's got it. "Anything else you've learned about how thinking strategically can help us as HR professionals? What else have you found useful?"

I nod. "Another pointer from Sasha: She advised me to think in terms of impact, not tasks. So, that means starting with 'What impact will this have on the business?' rather than starting with 'How much work will be involved?'"

"That's a great question to ask whenever we're considering a course of action. I'll use that one!" says Danielle.

"Anything else you can share? Is there anything that didn't go well?" Sam asks.

"Well," I think aloud. "I had concerns about staying authentic as I changed my focus and personal brand. I knew I wanted to be perceived as 'strategic,' but I wasn't sure how people would react. Surprisingly, the leadership team appreciates my new 'partnership' approach, and Rob, my assistant, is enjoying the opportunity it's giving him to step up and accept more responsibility.

"But I must admit, some people I've worked with for years have resisted the change, still wanting to drop in, whenever, and talk things over."

"How are you handling that?" Danielle asks.

"I'm still not 100% comfortable, but I guess it will take time. In the meantime, I've been asking people to work with Rob and framing it as helping him to develop. In most cases, they're okay with that. And I try to socialize more at lunch and during breaks, so people don't think I'm suddenly not interested in them. I'm still the Luisa they know."

"And love," smiles Danielle. I appreciate her empathy.

"There have been big changes in the way you think since the last time we met. What about speaking strategically? Are you doing that differently?" asks Sam, getting us back on track.

"Oh, yes," I smile. "My initial focus was on speaking strategically in the planning meeting, but as soon as I started thinking strategically, facing the future, and considering how I can add value to my colleagues and contribute to the success of our expansion, the way I speak just changed naturally."

"How so?" Danielle asks.

"In my meetings with the leadership team, I was asking questions that helped people frame their issues and focus on solutions. And a concept that Sasha told me about really helped me develop some skills in this area."

"Go on," Sam says. They're both intrigued.

"Consultative selling. It's a sales technique, but when applied to HR, it's more about facilitating problem-solving discussions within a team rather than trying to impose a solution.

"It's a collaborative approach to addressing business challenges. As an HR professional, you're essentially acting as an internal consultant."

"That sounds fascinating," says Danielle. "I'll look into it when I get back to the office."

I continue. "The goal is to ask the right questions to uncover underlying issues and encourage insights that lead to practical solutions. Instead of imposing predefined solutions, we guide discussions so people will share their perspectives.

"And that's precisely how I spoke at the big meeting. I prepared some questions to ask the leaders and made sure I had facts and data to share with the group in the discussions afterwards. I didn't impose any solutions, but when a group had fully considered an issue, I could suggest various options and help them reach a consensus."

"Brilliant," says Sam. "How was that approach received?"

"Perfectly!" I exclaim. "I was able to challenge without being threatening. Everyone could see that my questions were valid and aimed at finding the best solution. And when people challenged me, I shared the facts and data to support my opinions. They could agree or disagree, of course. But I was finally acting as a real partner in the business. It felt amazing!"

They both congratulate me.

"And what about the last piece in the puzzle? Have you translated your strategic thinking and speaking into strategic actions?" Sam asks.

"Absolutely!" I respond with confidence. "The roadmap became clear when I changed how I think and speak to face the future and align HR priorities with WFT's direction. So, for the last week or so, I've been working on collating all the needs that came out of the strategy meeting and developing a vision for HR's role in the next three years, with much more detail in the next 12 months.

"I'm now setting up a 'Talent Taskforce' with some of the key stakeholders on the leadership team to help guide the business in terms of resourcing and capability development as we transition to our new identity. I'll act as a facilitator and ensure that the business is intimately involved with the decisions we make.

"Well, that's certainly enough about me. I don't want to use up all the available time," I say in closing, feeling like I summarized my accomplishments well.

After a short pause, Danielle says, "Wow, Luisa! You've achieved so much since our last meeting! I'm in awe!"

I'm pleased that they share my feeling of success. I explain, "Once I internalized the Think-Speak-Act model, everything naturally fell into place. It was easy to partner with the other leaders and work with them to guide WFT towards a successful expansion."

I try to turn the attention to my colleagues. "So, Danielle, what's been happening with you? We're excited to hear. Are you still losing one of your team members?"

She laughs, so I guess her team is still intact.

"Let me go step by step, and I'll get to it," she explains. "Like you, when I returned to the office, I wanted to start 'being' strategic immediately. I wanted to think of a way to keep my current team, but I realized I had some work to do first.

"So, I went through the company's strategic business plan, line by line, until I knew every detail. Like you, Luisa, I prepared future-facing questions that would help me align my team's activities with the company's strategic business objectives.

"My approach made an impression on the COO because she didn't push the idea of me reducing my team when we met. Instead, I was able to speak to her about the contribution I could see HR making to the success of WMT. And she agreed to give me time to create an HR business plan that aligns with our objectives—while not letting me off the hook about cost reduction, of course!"

Sam interjects. "Yeah, that was something you were concerned about."

Danielle nods. "I was relieved that she was at least open to hearing my proposal. I put most of that down to the way I spoke strategically."

I ask, "Did you share the possibility of a reduction in the HR department with your team?"

"This was a dilemma for me, and I must admit I lost some sleep. I think of myself as open and transparent, but in the end, I decided against it.

"I was confident that I could get the changes I was proposing accepted, so upsetting them all about something that might never happen didn't seem the right thing to do. Instead, my challenge was to step up as their leader, to stop being so 'hands-on' and instead leverage their skills and enthusiasm to create an effective team structure to support the HR plan.

"Thinking strategically, it became my role to communicate my vision of HR's future contribution to the company so they could play their roles. I set up a planning meeting and led them through creating the HR strategic plan. So, after a quick brush-up on my rusty facilitation skills, we got together.

"I'd also been thinking about what our conference speaker, Simone Grant, had said about being authentic, so I was open about the fact that, until then, I'd acted as if the company's business plan had nothing to do with HR. And I apologized for that mistake. I learned a lot from their response: it doesn't hurt to admit you're vulnerable, and they were more than willing to open up and engage with the topic.

"Long story short, once they understood what the company was trying to achieve, they were ready to support every one of the five objectives. I continued encouraging them, empowering them to go away and come back with solutions and work with the rest of the company instead of staying 'siloed' in HR."

"Speaking strategically, then," Sam says with a smile, "it sounds like you rallied the troops!"

"I guess I did! Because they all worked like crazy over the coming week to collate ideas. I was also speaking to the key stakeholders to understand what they would need from HR in the future to achieve their objectives.

"And while they were busy doing their part, I continued thinking strategically. How could I ensure that my team would be in the best shape to deliver every goal we set?"

I'm beaming. "So, how did it go? I'm guessing you and your team killed it!"

Danielle grins. "Let's just say that we had the plan within the deadline, and the COO approved it!"

"Result!" says Sam.

"That's so awesome!" I say, echoing the congratulatory feelings.

Danielle continues. "The next challenge was to convince the leadership team. I was given 30 minutes in one of our meetings, but this was so important that I wasn't prepared to rush through my presentation without time for discussion. So I asked for an hour.

"It was time to speak strategically, to convince them that from now on, every HR initiative would be aligned with their business needs, address any concerns—and relaunch the 'Danielle brand' in the eyes of my peers. I got my 60 minutes. And by the end of the meeting, I'd gotten their approval."

"Fantastic!" I applaud.

Sam asks, "So what was your most important learning from all that?"

"As Luisa said, once I started thinking strategically and aligning my vision with that of the business, the direction followed naturally. And because it's so natural and logical, it's easy to speak about it. I didn't have to remind myself, 'Now, start speaking strategically, Danielle.' Because it happens naturally."

I'm delighted to learn how far she's come. "So, you've adjusted the way you think and speak. Have you had time yet for strategic action?"

She replies with excitement. "When I headed back to my team, I had two aims. First, to celebrate success! With their support, HR has evolved to add value to the business, and it's happened almost overnight! So, I stepped up again as their leader, praised them for their work, and painted a picture of an exciting future in their new roles. I've seen how important it is to speak about the future to galvanize a team into targeted action.

"Since then, I've been constantly in contact with my peers, acting as their partner to deliver what they need from HR—not today, but in the future. If anything, I've learned how much my new role was necessary because now they're confident that I'm 'in it' with them. Their challenges are now my opportunities. I'm becoming more of a trusted advisor."

Sam is enthusiastic. "It's great to hear about how much you've achieved in such a short time, Danielle, just by applying the Think-Speak-Act model."

Danielle smiles at us. "I'm so grateful I went to the conference that day and so glad I got to know you both. You've helped me so much. I've still got plenty to learn as VP of HR. I'm sure I'll slip up here and there, but I'm on the right track to achieving my ambition of becoming a CHRO.

"Well, that's enough about me. Sam, what's been happening with you?"

Sam takes a deep breath and focuses on his thoughts. "If you remember, by the end of our first meeting, I'd realized I'd been focusing on the wrong problem. I thought I needed help creating next year's HR budget.

"However, the real issue was that WAT had no clear strategic direction. That was what I needed to address, so my thinking shifted from tactical to strategic. My first task was to build a relationship with the CEO, but to do that, I had to pin him down. It took a lot of 6 a.m. breakfast meetings. But once we built trust, it wasn't hard to shift the conversations from yesterday to today—and start talking about the future."

I ask, "Was it really that easy? Did he let you set the agenda?"

"Not really," Sam admits. "I did far more listening than speaking. I occasionally asked strategic questions or answered his questions by referring to the future. But eventually, taking care to be logical and unemotional, I managed to gain his support for creating a new company-wide strategic plan that would align the whole company and get everyone working towards the same goals."

"I see." I nod. "So, what did you learn in this process? What advice would you give to someone in the same situation?"

"I'd say 'Speak the same language, see the big picture, and focus on the future.' Danielle said it just now—paint a picture of the various futures."

I agree. "Makes sense when you're supporting someone who always operates at the highest level. What else did you learn?"

"Seeing how he operates, I learned that once you commit to action, take action. It's the same in the military. When you decide on the right thing to do, based on facts, go ahead and do it. Don't delay. Don't wait for the ideal moment.

"For example, when my CEO realized it was time to communicate his Vision Statement and clarify our #1 Mission Statement, he went away, worked on it himself, and had it ready in days.

"And something else struck me as significant," Sam added. "When he talked to his team about the future, he took time to acknowledge how they'd gotten to where they are today. He didn't dismiss everything they'd already achieved. He told them he was proud. And his team appreciated that. I think it helped them be less resistant to the changes we were proposing.

"Now I understand that when you come into a new role and want to change things, it's essential to be mindful of how much effort people have put in and how proud they are of how far they've already come. It's essential to take time to acknowledge all that."

Danielle agrees, "That is so true! It's an insight into how to get people on your side when you're proposing a strategic change."

I encourage Sam to continue. I'm eager to hear whether he's delivered his budget.

"So yes, at a meeting arranged by the CEO, I got to speak strategically, and the leadership defined our objectives for the coming year. At that moment, I was finally accepted as part of the team."

"Congratulations!" Danielle and I both exclaim at the same time, as Sam continues.

"With a clear picture of what the business wants to achieve, it's been easy to put together a detailed HR strategy. With the rest of the business aligning their activities with the objectives they helped define, I've been working with them on what they'll need from HR. The result? My plan is confirmed, financed, and communicated across the company."

"Wow! That's so awesome. You clearly did an amazing job in thinking, speaking, and acting strategically, Sam!" Danielle exclaims with enthusiasm. "What else helped you?"

"Dexter Steele did play a part, I guess," Sam says enigmatically.

"Wait, the podcast guy?" I ask.

"No, the hologram!" Sam chuckles.

I have no idea what he's talking about, and Danielle looks befuddled. Sam explains briefly. Then he laughs. "Listen, we've all come a long way in a short time. We've put in the hard work to get to where we are today. Look at us! We're all confident, successful HR professionals."

"Don't forget about 'strong' and 'ambitious'," laughs Danielle.

And I have to add, "What about 'authentic' and 'empathetic'? And most of all, STRATEGIC!'"

Now we're all laughing.

Sam suggests, "What about if we all take a break and have lunch so we can continue our discussion? And I can tell you all about my encounter with the great man?"

We agree enthusiastically. And just like that, we're gone!

For the Reader: Ready to BE Strategic?

Based on the stories of Luisa, Danielle and Sam, and your reflections after each chapter, list how you're going to Think-Speak-Act strategically—and as a result, be strategic.

When am I going to start making the changes below?

THINKING STRATEGICALLY

Priority One

_____
_____
_____
_____
_____
_____
_____
_____
_____
_____

Priority Two

_____
_____
_____
_____
_____
_____
_____
_____
_____

Priority Three

_____

_____

_____

_____

_____

_____

_____

_____

SPEAKING STRATEGICALLY

Priority One

_____
_____
_____
_____
_____
_____
_____

Priority Two

_____
_____
_____
_____
_____
_____
_____

Priority Three

_____
_____
_____
_____
_____
_____
_____

ACTING STRATEGICALLY

Priority One

_____
_____
_____
_____
_____
_____
_____

Priority Two

_____
_____
_____
_____
_____
_____

Priority Three

_____
_____
_____
_____
_____
_____
_____

A NOTE FROM
THE AUTHOR

In today's rapidly evolving business landscape, HR professionals are increasingly called upon to embrace strategic leadership. While many are eager to make this shift, the path forward isn't always clear. I wrote this book to address that gap, offering practical, accessible tools to help HR professionals embody strategic thinking, speaking, and acting—without losing sight of their vital operational roles.

HR professionals, particularly in small to midsize companies, often juggle many responsibilities and lack direct guidance on how to become more strategic. Yet, the ability to seamlessly blend operational efficiency with strategic foresight is what sets successful HR leaders apart. Through the stories of Louisa, Danielle, and Sam, I've illustrated the challenges many HR professionals face and provided practical tools to help you navigate the balance between strategic thinking and operational execution.

As the world continues to change, the need for strategic HR leadership grows even more vital. I'd like to leave you with a thought from Mahatma Gandhi: "Your beliefs become your thoughts, your thoughts become your words, your words become your actions, your actions become your habits, your habits become your values, your values become your destiny." These words perfectly encapsulate how thinking, speaking, and acting strategically are interconnected and how these elements can shape not only your career but also your impact on the organization.

I encourage you to take these ideas forward and embrace your evolution as a strategic leader. As you continue on this journey, I would love to stay connected. Please reach out to me on LinkedIn to share your insights, experiences, or questions. If this book has been helpful to you, I invite you to leave a review so we can continue the conversation on how HR professionals can lead strategically in today's dynamic business world. Let's keep the dialogue going!

Warm regards,
Nadine Stead Ontiveros

ACKNOWLEDGEMENTS

Writing this book has been a journey of reflection, growth, and collaboration, and I am deeply grateful to those who have supported and inspired me along the way. It has been a creative journey, taking an idea and turning it into a reality—one that I couldn't have completed without the encouragement and belief of those around me.

To my husband, parents, and children—thank you for your constant encouragement and belief in me. Your unwavering support has given me the strength and confidence to bring this book to life, and I am forever grateful for the love and inspiration you've provided.

To my friends and colleagues, your support and encouragement have been my anchor. Your belief in me has fueled my passion and kept me motivated through every stage of this project. Thank you for the countless conversations, brainstorming sessions, and the endless patience you've shown.

To my professional peers, your insights and feedback have been invaluable. I am grateful for the stimulating discussions and collaborative spirit that have shaped the direction of this book and contributed significantly to its development.

A heartfelt thank you to the incredible team of editors, publishers, formatters, and designers. Your expertise and dedication have brought this book to life, and I couldn't have done it without your meticulous work and creative vision.

To everyone I've collaborated with over the years, thank you for sharing your knowledge and experiences, which have enriched my understanding and shaped my own growth. Our collective learning and partnerships have been instrumental in my journey and this book's creation.

Finally, to all those who have been part of this endeavor, your support has been a crucial element in the completion of this book. I look forward to continuing this journey together and hope that this book serves as a valuable resource and source of inspiration for you.